MEDIEVAL SEXUALITY

GARLAND MEDIEVAL BIBLIOGRAPHIES
(VOL. 5)

GARLAND REFERENCE LIBRARY
OF SOCIAL SCIENCE
(VOL. 565)

GARLAND MEDIEVAL BIBLIOGRAPHIES

1. *Europe in Transition: A Select, Annotated Bibliography of the Twelfth-Century Renaissance*
   Chris D. Ferguson

2. *Medieval English Drama: An Annotated Bibliography of Recent Criticism*
   Sidney E. Berger

3. *François Villon: A Bibliography*
   Robert D. Peckham

4. *Music and Literature in the Middle Ages: An Annotated Bibliography*
   Margaret Louise Switten

5. *Medieval Sexuality: A Research Guide*
   Joyce E. Salisbury

MEDIEVAL SEXUALITY
A Research Guide

Joyce E. Salisbury

GARLAND PUBLISHING, INC. • NEW YORK & LONDON
1990

Library of Congress Cataloging-in-Publication Data

Salisbury, Joyce E.
Medieval sexuality: a research guide / Joyce E. Salisbury.
p. cm. — (Garland medieval bibliographies; vol. 5)
(Garland reference library of social science; vol. 565)
ISBN 0–8240–7642–7 (alk. paper)
I. Sex customs—Europe—History—Bibliography. 2. Europe—Social conditions—To 1492—Bibliography. 3. Marriage customs and rites, Medieval—Bibliography. I. Title. II. Series. III. Series: Garland reference library of social science; v. 565.
Z7164.S42S24 1990
[HQ14]
016.3067'094—dc20 89–48357
CIP

Printed on acid-free, 250-year-life paper
Manufactured in the United States of America

TO

ROBERT E. SALISBURY

CONTENTS

PREFACE

Before beginning this bibliography on medieval sexuality, I had to define the term "sexuality" and restrict the topic to useful proportions. Sexuality is interwoven with a number of other subjects, marriage, family, romance, love, erotic sensibilities, even religious passion. Studies on all of those topics would certainly illuminate our shadowy sexual past, but a bibliography covering all those areas would simply be an invitation to consult a full bibliography of all medieval materials.

To provide a practical guide, I have made a number of restrictions. I have eliminated works on marriage and family, except where the work specifically addresses marital intercourse. Of course, I recognize the close relationship between the two subjects, and works like James Brundage's *Law, Sex, and Christian Society in Medieval Europe* (item 323) do an excellent job of integrating the two subjects. However, there are a number of bibliographies available on marriage and the family, and it would be voluminous and not necessarily useful to reproduce them here. See for example, Joan Aldous and Reuben Hill, *International Bibliography of Research in Marriage and the Family* (Minneapolis, Univ. of Minnesota Press, 1967), or Michael M. Sheehan, *Family and Marriage in Medieval Europe: A Working Bibliography* (item 501). The latter is included in this bibliography because it contains a section on attitudes toward sexuality.

Love was a thornier issue. Historical and literary analyses from the twelfth century onward include discussions on what has been called "courtly love," which may or may not have involved sexual consummation. I have made no attempt to include primary and secondary works that deal with courtly love, platonic love, or romance in the abstract. I have restricted my study to works that refer to love consummated in some fashion. (This raises the question of what constitutes "consummation," and I can only admit that is a judgment call.)

Useful in developing a working definition of sexuality for this bibliography, was John E. Keller's identification (in his introduction to Juan Ruiz's *Book of Good Love*, item 161) of three philosophies of love that existed in medieval Spain (as well as the rest of Europe). One is courtly love ("in its purest form spiritual and lacking in physical contact"), another is Ovidian love ("carnal and earthly"), and finally, an "even more carnal kind of love that was based upon the doctrine of plenitude" (p. xxiii). I have included works that reveal the latter two kinds of love. This selection means that I have excluded important works on romance and love, like those of C. S. Lewis, *The Allegory of Love: A Study in Medieval Tradition* (London: Oxford University Press, 1959) and Denis de Rougement, *Love in the Western World,* translated by Montgomery Belgion (New York: Pantheon, 1956). I have also excluded works like Felix Schlösser, *Andreas Capellanus: Seine Minnelehre und das Christliche Weltbild um 1200* (Bonn, H. Bouvier, 1960), who argues at length that courtly love has nothing to do with consummation. I do not claim that unconsummated love is unimportant. In fact, it no doubt deserves a bibliography of its own. That would be a different book, not this one.

The logic I used to exclude courtly love also requires me to exclude religious love, and the often erotic language with which such love is expressed. My background in religious history made this a difficult decision. Much of the language of the mystics, for example, is beautiful, erotic, and expressive of the sexual attitudes of the believer. However, such works might well join a bibliography of courtly and platonic love as part of expressions of unconsummated (sublimated?) desire.

This is perhaps enough on what I eliminated. I have included any work that discusses or describes sexual contact or attitudes toward sexual contact. Within this definition, I have incorporated works dealing with intercourse, fornication, adultery, homosexuality, prostitution, bestiality, or any activities related to these themes. I have also included many works of medieval gynecology, which we do not necessarily consider sexual, yet which medieval people did. Conversely, people in the Middle Ages did not necessarily consider transvestism a sexual issue, but since we in the twentieth century often do, I have included works on people who cross-dressed. I can only hope that this selection will help direct scholars to materials that will forward knowledge in this field of human experience.

Historians of sexuality sometimes confront the question of whether to study attitudes toward sexuality or sexual practices (the former has been viewed as the most legitimate, or at least the least prurient). I have approached this bibliography with the assumption that both are legitimate and, indeed, related. Therefore, I have included sources that simply refer to sexual practices, in addition to those that express an opinion about sex and sexuality.

In addition to content considerations and restrictions, I had to make choices about time and geography. There is, of course, no clear-cut time period that everyone can agree is medieval, so in this I had to be fairly arbitrary. For the secular sources, I began with about the fifth century. For Christian sources, however, I looked at materials from the late antique, beginning as early as the second century. Christian patristic works from that period were central in shaping subsequent medieval thought, so I have included them here. There are similar problems with the ending date of the Middle Ages. I have ended in Italy at 1375 (the death of Boccaccio, a convenient and customary turning point). In the north, which experienced the Renaissance later, I have included works through the middle of the fifteenth century.

Questions of chronology also influenced content issues. I have included works on sex related to satanism, witchcraft, and demonology. There are medieval beginnings to these activities, for example, the first woman to be charged with intercourse with a demon seems to have taken place in Toulouse in 1275. However, these trends only came to full development after 1400. The high point for sexual satanism was the seventeenth century, well out of the period under discussion in this research guide. The books included here note the medieval origins of such activities.

I have further limited this bibliography to Western Europe, and included works in Spanish, Portuguese,

French, Italian, and German in addition to English. Studies of Spain yield some material on Arabic and Hebrew erotic poetry and philosophy, but this bibliography does not pretend to exhaust those subjects. My language skills did not permit an extensive study of the Arabic and Hebrew sources, but the works included here will direct the interested reader to further studies.

The book is organized in two main divisions, primary and secondary sources, and the entries are arranged alphabetically within each chapter. Most of the entries are annotated to indicate the kind of information about sexuality that is available in the source. The only entries that lack annotations are those I found referred to in at least one secondary work on the subject, yet was unable to obtain.

The primary sources are further subdivided by discipline. There are chapters on sources from history, law, literature, religion, and science. Many of the primary sources mentioned in the bibliography have only a small mention of sexual incidents, but that is the way research on medieval sexuality will have to be built. Nice long tracts dealing directly with the subject are unfortunately rare. I do not begin to claim that the primary sources listed here exhaust the subject. These provide a starting point, and indicate the kind of information on sexuality found in the various kinds of sources. The introductory paragraphs that precede each primary source chapter discuss further the nature of the sources and the information they yield. I made no attempt to list all the editions and translations of a particular source. There are other bibliographies that provide that kind of information. (A fine example is János M. Bak. *Medieval Narrative Sources* [New York: Garland Publishing, Inc., 1987] for historical sources.) Instead I have listed an accessible edition and/or translation of a source that contains sexual information. When I have listed two or more versions of one source, it is because they each provide different information about sexuality, whether in the introductions or in the nature of the translations.

The secondary sources are simply divided between books and articles. Too many works draw from many disciplines to make any organization by primary source feasible. All the works deal directly with some aspect of sexuality as I have defined it above. In some cases, only a portion of a book might touch on sexuality, and the annotation will indicate the relevant portions. I have included some secondary works that may not discuss sexuality directly, but comment on the most important of the primary sources that do (such as Alan of Lille, Peter Damian, Hincmar of Reims or *Roman de la Rose*).

All the items are numbered, and there are cross-references to the item numbers throughout the annotations. I have cross-referenced only those works that refer directly to one another. Works that are related in theme may be traced in the subject index. I have tried to make that index comprehensive, referring to literary or historical topics (i.e., Chaucer or prostitution) and to sexual activities (i.e., rape or sodomy). In addition to the subject index, I have provided one index of authors, editors and translators, and another index of centuries, in which the primary sources are listed chronologically. All are indexed by item number.

There are few existing bibliographies that I could consult for this work. Vern L. Bullough's *Bibliography of Prostitution* (item 325) was a useful starting point for that subject. Most of my references, however, came from the bibliographies and notes of the major works on the various subjects. Some works are particularly rich in citations, and further studies must begin with them. For homosexuality, see John Boswell's work (item 310), for prostitution, Leah L. Otis (item 460), for medicine, Danielle Jacquart (item 408), for legal sources, James Brundage (item 323) and Pierre Payer's work on penitentials (item 468), and for early religious sources, Peter Brown (item 321).

These works and many others have led me to the works listed in this bibliography. I am certain I could have included others, yet I believe there is enough here to help medievalists further an interesting, important, and growing field of study.

ACKNOWLEDGMENTS

It would have been impossible to complete a project of such diversity without generous help from colleagues. I cannot acknowledge everyone who offered me direction and anecdotes. However, I do want specifically to mention Professor James Brundage of the University of Wisconsin - Milwaukee, Professor Michael Sheehan of the Pontifical Institute in Toronto, Professor Joan Cadden of Kenyon College, and Professor Christopher Kleinhenz of the University of Wisconsin - Madison for generously sharing their extensive bibliographies, which represent years of work in the field. Any omissions of significant works from my bibliography derive from my own shortcomings, not from these thorough scholars.

This work has been also helped by people at my own institution. Kurt Treptow and Madellon Kohler-Busch proved excellent research assistants. Anyone who has done research at small institutions will appreciate my debt to our inter-library loan librarian, Deb Grothman.

The Newberry Library supported and forwarded this project by awarding me a fellowship to use their collection. The extensive medieval holdings, the staff of scholars, and the other fellows in residence all were an indispensable resource.

Finally, the dedication is for my father. Not only has he been encouraging and supportive over the years, but with expert guidance, he brought me painlessly into the computer age so that I could produce a work like this.

INTRODUCTION

The study of the history of sexuality is not new, yet periodically it receives renewed attention. Sexuality is so intimately associated with what it means to be human, that theologians, philosophers, historians, and others who explore the human condition turn their attention to how we view our sexual selves. In the 1980's historians are bringing new questions and methods to the study of sexuality and sexual attitudes. There are new journals dedicated to the subject and new works coming out regularly; this development will certainly continue into the 1990's.

Until recently, the main questions we have asked concern repression. Those studying sexuality have assumed we are burdened with repression, and look for the origins of those restraints. They have tried to determine which historical period or event to blame for the sexual burden we bear. Michel Foucault (see item 377) is one of the fathers of the philosophical/ historical studies on the subject of sexuality. He redefined the question a bit by asking not why we are repressed, but why we argue with such passion that we are repressed. Furthermore, he saw studies of sexuality as attempts to free ourselves from the previous repression (pp. 6-8). His conclusions regarding the development of sexual attitudes have been superceded, yet his observation that since the sixteenth century, sexuality has not been silenced, but been discussed endlessly (p. 13) is certainly true. We may be repressed, but we have remained prolifically interested in the phenomenon.

Each generation has focused on different aspects of the question of sexuality. In the nineteenth century, societies were worried about prostitution and venereal disease, and historians reflected that interest by writing (with apologies in the introductions) about the history of prostitution and venereal disease. See, for examples, Heinrich Lippert (item 22), Hippolyte Mireur (item 23), or L. le Pilleur (item 26).

Nineteenth-century medievalists made great progress in editing primary sources. However, their editions and translations often reflected their views on sexuality by imposing their values on the sources. The indexes usually do not cite information on sexual attitudes or acts, even when the source contains it. (The twentieth century is not exempt from such omissions, either. For example, patristic material that deals explicitly with sexuality is not indexed for it. One example is the Fathers of the Church edition of Augustine, *Against Julian*,item 182.) Some nineteenth-century editions omitted sexually explicit material altogether. For example, in the *Institutes of the Coenobia* by John Cassian, the translators in the Nicene and Post-Nicene Fathers series omitted Book VI, saying "We have thought best to omit altogether the translation of this book" (p. 248. John Cassian "Institutes of the Coenobia" *Nicene and Post-Nicene Fathers,* 2nd ser. vol. 11. Translated by P. Schaff and H. Wace. New York: The Christian Literature Co., 1894). The full text is edited in item 190.

At times, studies have reflected an interest in pornography. A number of works have been published (particularly in the 1930's) on aspects of the history of sexuality that claimed to be scholarly, yet were designed to be titillating rather than historically accurate. See, for example, Emíle Laurent, *Magica Sexualis* (item 423). Such works brought history to the service of sexuality.

The late 1960's and early 1970's was another period of interest in the history of sexuality. Increased awareness of homosexuality and the Gay Rights movement led to studies of the history of homosexuality. Some of the early works merely sought to demonstrate that homosexuality existed in the Middle Ages, and this approach led to some superficial and ahistorical works like James Graham's *The Homosexual Kings of England* (item 391), or A.L. Rowse, *Homosexuals in History* (item 488). The field became more sophisticated, however, and studies like John Boswell's (item 310), while controversial, made a solid contribution not only to our understanding of historical homosexuality, but to attitudes toward sexuality in general. The reader will note that there are many works on homosexuality, and this reflects the early and sustained interest in the topic.

Studies on homosexuality have focused on changing attitudes towards homosexuals and homosexual acts (recalling Foucault's discussion of interest in the history of repression). As I indicated in the Preface, this bibliography includes attention to sexual acts in addition to attitudes, and the field of homosexual history provides an example of changing practices over time. The sources show that medieval references to homosexual activity focus on anal intercourse over oral intercourse. (There is virtually no mention of the latter). Anal intercourse appears in various sources: 1) Scandinavian sources refer to the activity and it has been analyzed in some fine studies (notably, P. M. Sorensen, item 506). 2) Fabliaux refer to it fairly often in a comic fashion, and contain no references to oral sex in this comic tradition. 3) Peter Damian in his Book of Gomorrah (item 225) lists four types of homosexual activity and doesn't refer to oral sex. These references focus on practices, yet shed light on sexual attitudes. It remains for future historians to explain such developments.

Interest in Women's Studies brought an increase in studies of families, children, and sexuality. Although sexuality is not a single-gender issue, much work on the history of sexuality remains tied to women's studies, perhaps perpetuating the medieval idea that sexuality is quintessentially women's provence. More recent work like that of Peter Brown (item 321) is subsuming the history of sexuality within the larger issue of the history of attitudes toward the body. This approach seems to have broken the gender boundaries, but it remains to be seen whether that trend continues.

Medievalists are relatively new to the field of the history of sexuality. There has been more work done on ancient, Renaissance or early modern attitudes and practices than on medieval ones. This is probably due to the number of and accessibility of sources. For the Middle Ages, most work has been done using medical and religious sources. In the medical sources, one finds the most direct references to sexuality, and much fine analysis has been done (most recently is that of Danielle Jacquart, item 408).

The religious sources have been extensively used in part because the material is relatively abundant. The Church was interested in morality, and this interest led to commentary and legislation on sexual behavior. Peter Brown (item 321) and James Brundage (item 323) are but two examples of historians who have used the plentiful ecclesiastical material. Another probable reason for the research on religious attitudes is our abiding interest in the history of repression as much as the history of sexuality. The Catholic church has been both blamed for and absolved of imposition of sexual repression. Many of the studies have considered that question, and the answers are as varied as the studies. Nevertheless, the search for the origins of repression, have led historians to mine the ecclesiastical sources.

Studies of the religious sources have continued the patristic speculations about whether sex is intrinsically good or evil. This seems a rather remarkable question, yet theologians still debate it (see John Dedek's article, items 598, and 600, for examples), and it has shaped a number of the historical studies.

While studies in the fields of religion and medicine have forwarded our understanding considerably, they are nevertheless specialized studies, raising the question of how widely the conclusions may be applied. Much more work needs to be done using other kinds of sources before generalizations may be made about medieval sexuality, whether practices or attitudes. This bibliography includes various types of sources to provide a beginning point for further studies. Each type presents its own problems. Historical sources do not deal with the subject systematically. The information they contain is scanty and scattered, so it is a challenge to use the historical anecdotes in any comprehensive way. The literary sources pose the perennial problem of whether art is an accurate mirror of life. In spite of these problems, research that combines the most varied information will surely yield the fullest results. Further studies will help us to understand the attitudes toward sexuality that still influence us millennia after the cultures that spawned them passed away.

PRIMARY SOURCES

PRIMARY SOURCES

HISTORY

Historical sources include chronicles, documents and letters. These have not been used in any systematic way for the study of sexuality probably because information on sexuality within them is scarce and scattered. Most of the historical sources mention sexual incidents as scandals or anecdotes within a larger narrative. Some (like Gerald of Wales or William of Malmesbury) pass on rumors without any attempt to determine their accuracy, and this casual attitude toward truth has also no doubt made historians reluctant to depend upon their accounts to develop a history of sexuality. Nevertheless, the way scandals were reported and the selection of anecdotes (real or not) reveals at least the chroniclers' attitudes toward sexuality. The infrequency with which historians of sexuality have used these materials means I did not have many citations from which to draw as I was compiling this section. Thus my list of historical sources is the least comprehensive of all these chapters of primary sources. It must only serve as a beginning.

1. Abelard, Peter. *Historia Calamitatum: The Story of My Misfortunes*. Translated by H.A. Bellows. New York: William Edwin Rudge, 1922.

   Translates Abelard's account of his affair with Héloïse and his castration. Twelfth century.

2. Adam of Bremen. *History of the Archbishop of Hamburg-Bremen*. Translated by Francis J.

Ischan. New York: Columbia University Press, 1959.

Comments on the reputed extraordinary sexual capacity of Swedes. Eleventh century.

3. Aelred of Rievaulx. "Aelred of Rievaulx and the Nun of Watton." Translated by Giles Constable. *Medieval Women.* Edited by Derek Baker. Oxford: Basil Blackwell, 1978, pp. 205-26.

Offers a translation of an account of seduction and castration for revenge. Twelfth century.

4. Azais, J., ed. "Documents inédits du XIVe siècle sur les Filles ou Femmes de Mauvaise Vie." *Bulletin de la Société Archéologique de Béziers* 1st ser. 2 (1837): 255-323.

Edits documents on the history of prostitution. Fourteenth century.

5. "The Book of Hyde." *The Church Historians of England,* vol.2, part II. Edited by J. Stevenson. London: Seeleys, 1854, pp. 483-520.

Describes incubi who gathered sperm from humans, then had intercourse with women and impregnated them. Compiled in the fourteenth century.

* Buttitta, Antonio, ed. *Classici della Cultura Siciliana.* Cited below as item 336.

Includes documents on the history of prostitution in Sicily.

6. Calza, Carlo, ed. "Documenti inediti sulla Prostituzione tratti dagli Archivii della Repubblica Veneta." *Giornale Italiano delle Malattie Veneree e della Pelle* 5 (1869): Part 1: 305-20,365-72; Part 2: 119-25,247-55,316-19.

Collects documents on the history of prostitution in Venice.

7. Febretti, Ariodante, ed. *La Prostituzione in Perugia nei Secoli XIV, XV e XVI: Documenti editii.* Torino: Coi tipi privati dell'editore, 1890.

Collects documents on the history of prostitution in Perugia. Fourteenth and fifteenth centuries.

8. Froissart, Jean. *Chronicles.* Translated by G. Brereton. New York: Penguin, 1968.

Relates an account of the reign of Edward II, and his reputation for homosexuality. Describes the castration and execution of the king's accused lover. Also describes the rapes that took place during the violence of the Jacquerie. Late fourteenth century.

9. Galbraith, V.H., ed. *The Anonimalle Chronicle, 1333-1381.* New York: Barnes & Noble, 1970.

Describes the peasant uprising in 1381 that destroyed a house of prostitution in Southwark, outside London. Late fourteenth century.

10. Giraldus Cambrensis. "Gemma Ecclesiastica." *Opera* 8 vols. Edited by J.S. Brewer and J.F. Dimrock. London: Rerum Britannicarum Medii Aevi Scriptores, 1861-91, vol. 2, pp. 216-17.

Describes King Louis VII's physician's advice that he should have intercourse to cure himself of a medical problem. His cure was accomplished. Late twelfth century.

11. ——. *The Historical Works of Giraldus Cambrensis.* Edited by Thomas Wright. Translated by T. Forester & P.C. Hoare. London: George Bell & Sons, 1887.

Includes translations of "Topography of Ireland," "History of the Conquest of Ireland," "Itinerary through Wales," and "Description of Wales." Offers accounts of bestiality, demon intercourse, adultery and incest. Late twelfth century.

12. ——. *A Journey Through Wales.* Translated by L. Thorpe. New York: Penguin, 1978.

Includes accounts of bestiality. Late twelfth century.

13. ——. *Topography of Ireland.* Translated by J.J. O'Meare. New York: Penguin, 1982.

Includes accounts of bestiality and incest. Late twelfth century.

14. Guibert of Nogent. *Self and Society in Medieval France: The Memoirs of Abbot Guibert of Nogent.* Edited by John F. Benton. New York: Harper Torchbooks, 1970.

Presents an unusually personal account of the events observed by the Abbot, within which he vividly expresses his views of sexuality, recounting his father's impotence, his mother's purity, his own profound sense of sexual shame, and his denunciations of sexual depravity. Early twelfth century.

15. Henry of Huntingdon. *History of England.* Translated by T. Forester. London: Henry G. Bohn, 1853.

Relates the scandal in 1123 of a cardinal who, after preaching harshly against priests with concubines, was caught with a prostitute. Early twelfth century.

16. Ibn Fadhlan, Ahmad. *Ibn Fadlan's Reisebericht.* Edited by A. Zeki Validi Togan. Leipzig: Kommissionsverlag F.A. Brockhaus, 1939.

Describes casual sexual morality of northmen, including acceptance of public intercourse. See item 17 for more accessible excerpts. Tenth century.

17. ——. "Observations on the Manners and Customs of the Northmen Encamped on the Volga." *A Reader in General Anthropology.* Edited by Carleton S. Coon. New York: Henry Holt, 1948, pp. 410-16.

Offers excerpts from the source that describes Nordic sexual morality. Compare with item 16. Tenth century.

18. Ingulf. "The History of Ingulf." *The Church Historians of England,* vol. 2, part II. Translated by J. Stevenson. London: Seeleys, 1854, pp. 565-726.

Incorporates the early laws of William the Conqueror into the Chronicle. These laws contain penalties for rape and adultery. Ingulf also tells of King Eadwig's "licentious youth," and notes that Queen Ethelfleda renounced sexual intercourse and then became "as a man." Twelfth century.

19. Jacques de Vitry. *Historia Occidentalis.* Edited by J. F. Hinnebusch. Fribourg: University Press, 1972.

Discusses with horror the prostitutes of the city of Paris. Early thirteenth-century.

20. Jean de Joinville. "The Life of St. Louis." *Chronicles of the Crusades.* Translated by M.R.B. Shaw. New York: Penguin Classics, 1963.

Includes a description of Louis' efforts to control prostitution in France. Fourteenth century.

21. John of Wallingford. "Chronicle." *The Church Historians of England,* vol. 2. Translated by Joseph Stevenson. London: Seeleys, 1854, pp. 523-64.

Relates a history of Anglo-Saxon England, and includes descriptions of rapes after battles, King Alfred's violation of virgins, Eadwin's seduction of mother and daughter, and other such incidents woven throughout the narrative.

22. Lippert, Heinrich, ed. *Die Prostitution in Hamburg.* Hamburg: B.S. Berendsohn, 1848.

Collects documents on the history of prostitution in Hamburg.

23. Mireur, Hippolyte, ed. *La Prostitution à Marseille. Histoire, Administration et Police, Hygiene.* Paris: E. Dentu, 1882.

Collects documents on the history of prostitution and venereal disease in Marseille.

24. Norman Anonymous. *Die Texte des Normannischen Anonymus*. Edited by Franz Karl Pellens. Wiesbaden: Steiner Verlag, 1966.

Defends clerical marriage, and in doing so, the Norman departed from the Augustinian view of sex and argued that carnal birth and human sexuality, along with human nature were all good. Eleventh century.

25. Ordericus Vitalis. *Ecclesiastical History,* 4 vols. Edited by M. Chibnall. Oxford: Clarendon Press, 1969-80.

Accuses the English court after William the Conqueror of sexual license, homosexuality, effeminacy, and general decadence. Also see Book IV, in which Norman women demanded that William release their husbands so they could return to Normandy to satisfy their sexual needs. Twelfth century.

26. Pilleur, L. le, ed. *La Prostitution du XIIIe au XVIIe siècle, Documents tiré des Archivists d'Avignon.* Paris: H. Champignon, 1908.

Collects documents from Provence and Besançon on the history of prostitution and venereal disease.

27. Radice, Betty, trans. *The Letters of Abelard and Heloise.* New York: Penguin, 1981.

Contains a translation of the letters exchanged between Heloise and Abelard, in which they recall their sexual life. Also provides a translation of Abelard's *Historia Calamitatum* (compare with item 1).

28. Richard of Devizes. *The Chronicle of Richard of Devizes of the Time of King Richard the First.* Translated by John T. Appleby. New York: Thomas Nelson & Sons, Ltd., 1963.

Offers a witty description of London which lists the unsavory characters one might find in the city. In his list, Richard names pederasts, pimps, homosexuals and others. This narrative has been used to provide evidence for the existence of certain sexual practices in twelfth-century London. The chronicle should be used cautiously, for Richard could be drawing from classical formulaic critiques of society. Appleby's edition is very useful, for it provides the original Latin with an English translation. See also, Warren Johansson, item 662, for a discussion of Appleby's translation of the sexual terms. Twelfth century.

29. Roger of Hovedon. *Annals of Roger de Hovedon.* Edited by H.T. Riley. London: H. G. Bohn, 1853.

Tells of a physician's prescription to Thomas, Archbishop of York, that he would die if he did not have intercourse with a woman. He chose death. Also describes clergy being forced to give up their wives and mistresses in 1108, and tells of possible castration as a penalty for coin debasement. Late twelfth century.

* Rossiaud, Jacques, ed. *Medieval Prostitution.* Cited below as item 485.

Collects documents related to prostitution in an appendix.

30. Salimbene de Adam. *The Chronicle of Salimbene de Adam* Translated by Joseph L. Baird, *et al.* Binghamton,NY: Medieval and Renaissance Texts and Studies, 1986.

Presents a complete and careful translation of the Franciscan's chronicle, with all its sexual and scatological details that Coulton (Item 31) omitted in his earlier, partial translation. A welcome contribution to scholarship. Thirteenth century.

31. Salimbene de Adam. *From St. Francis to Dante.* Translated by G.G. Coulton, Philadelphia: University of Pennsylvania Press, 1972.

Presents excerpts of translations from the Chronicle of the Franciscan Salimbene. In Appendix C, Coulton provides the Latin edition of passages he chose not to translate. Among these are those that contain references to pederasty. Thirteenth century.

32. Saxo Grammaticus. *Saxonis Grammatici Historiae Danicae Lib. XVI*. Sorae: Typis et sumptibus J. Moltkenii, 1644.

Claims that a group of people were punished for sexual sins by being inseparably joined in the act of intercourse, and displayed in such a condition for public ridicule. Early thirteenth century.

33. Schrank, Josef, ed. *Die Prostitution in Wien in Historischer, Administrativer und Hygienischer Beziehung*. Vienna: Selbstverlag des Verfassers, 1886.

Collects local documents on the history of prostitution and venereal disease in Vienna.

34. Stevenson, Joseph, ed. *Chronicon de Lanercost*. Edinburgh: Impressum Edinburgi, 1839.

Describes people's reliance on phallic worship during an epidemic of cattle disease in 1268. Thirteenth century.

35. Sulpicius Severus. "The Sacred History." *Nicene and Post-Nicene Fathers of the Christian Church*, vol. 11. Translated by P. Schaff and H. Wace. New York: Christian Literature Co., 1894, pp. 71-122.

Tells of women who traveled with the heretic, Priscillian, and of one who procured an abortion after getting pregnant through adultery with the heresiarch. Late fourth/early fifth century.

36. Walter de Hemingburghe. *Chronica Domini Walterus de Hemingburghe*. Edited by R. Claude Hamilton. London: Royal Historical Society, 1847.

Describes a prostitute soliciting on the streets of London, and tells of King John's fornication with his vassals' wives. Late thirteenth/early fourteenth century.

37. William of Malmesbury. *Gesta Regum Anglorum*. 2 vols. Vaduz: Kraus Reprint Ltd., 1964.

Includes stories of corrupt monks, and various anecdotes of sexual sins in the English court, for example, general licentiousness during the reign of William Rufus, the incest of Eadbald, adultery of King Philip, and other such accounts. Twelfth century.

PRIMARY SOURCES

LAW

Legal sources are particularly rich in information on sexuality throughout the Middle Ages. The early Germanic laws regulated adultery and other sexual crimes. Religious penitentials continued and expanded such regulation. Legal attention to sexual matters increased with the development of canon law, and moral legislation was secularized with the growth of royal law codes. The sources listed below include secular and ecclesiastical laws, as well as trial records and local statutes and regulations. This bibliography does not include manuscript collections, which a full study of legal sources requires. The work of James Brundage (item 323) is an indispensable guide to the canon law sources, and Pierre Payer's work (item 468) covers the penitentials. There are no comparable comprehensive guides to the secular legal sources.

38. Alexander of Hales. *Summa Theologiae...cura PP. Collegii S. Bonaventurae. 4 vols.* Quaracchi: Ex Typographia Colleggii S.Bon., 1924-48.

    Argues (in volume 2) that intercourse from the rear was unnatural and a serious sin. Thirteenth century.

39. Alvarus Pelagius. *De Planctu Ecclesiae.* Venice: n.p., 1560.

    Contains references to the use of birth control (See especially chapter iii). Fourteenth century.

40. Andreae, Joannes. *Summa de Sponsalibus et Matrimoniis*. Padua: Bernardinus Celerius, 1748.

Provides a commentary on canon law that makes a contribution to the theories of sexuality in marriage. Fourteenth century.

41. Attenborough, F.L., ed. *The Laws of the Earliest English Kings*. New York: AMS Press, 1974.

Contains the references to adultery in the earliest English laws. Includes the Kentish laws, those of Ine and Alfred, charters of the Danes and laws of Edward the Elder and Aethelsten. Particularly useful is the index, which guides one to all the references to adultery.

42. Bieler, L., ed. *The Irish Penitentials*. Dublin: Scriptores Latini Hiberniae, 1963.

43. Boretius, A., ed. "Ansegisi abbatis capitularium collectio." *Monumenta Germaniae Historica, Legum, Sectio II*, vol. 1, Hanover: Impensis bibliopolii Hahniani, 1883, p. 382.

Compiles previous capitularies. Contains references to homosexuality, bestiality and other sexual topics. Also available in Migne, *Patrologiae Cursus Completus, Series Latina 97,* 513ff. Ninth century.

44. ——. "Capitularia Regum Francorum." *Monumenta Germaniae Historica Legum Sectio II,* vol. 1. Hanover: Impensis bibliopolii Hahniani, 1883, pp. 297-98.

Contains a capitulary of Louis the Pious against prostitutes. Ninth century.

45. ——. "Capitularia regum francorum." *Monumenta Germaniae Historica, Legum Sectio II,* vol. 1, no. 22. Hanover: Impensis bibliopolii Hahniani, 1883, pp. 295-96.

Reaffirms the Council of Ancyra's prohibitions against homosexuality and bestiality. Eighth century.

46. Bracton, Henricus. *De Legibus et Consuetudinibus Angliae*. Edited by G.E. Woodbine. Cambridge: Cambridge University Press, 1968.

Provides a summary of laws as they had developed by the mid-thirteenth century. Stressed that intention was necessary for offense, a theme that had implications for sexual faults. Thirteenth century.

47. Britton, John. *Britton.* Edited by Francis Morgan Nichols. Oxford: Clarendon Press, 1865.

Presents a British vernacular law code containing penalties for "unnatural" sex acts, including homosexuality and bestiality. Early fourteenth century.

48. Burchard of Worms. "Decretorum." *Patrologiae Cursus Completus, Series Latina 140*. Edited by Migne. Belgium: Brepols, 1844-55 pp. 537-1058.

Collects penitential canons. See chapter 7 on incest, chapter 9 on marriage, chapter 17 on fornication, and chapter 19 on penitence. See also H.J. Schmitz (item 49) for another edition of the collection. Eleventh century.

49. ——. "Decretum." *Die Bussbucher und das kanonische Bussverfahren nach handschriftlichen Quellen dargestellt.* Edited by Hermann J. Schmitz. Düsseldorff: L. Schwann, 1898.

Offers a more careful edition than that of Migne (item 48). Eleventh century.

50. Cam, H.M., ed. *The London Eyre of 1321.* London: Quaritch, 1968.

Provides an edition and translation that describes sexual offenses such as adultery, fornication, etc. Fourteenth century.

51. Clanchy, M.T., ed. *Roll and Writ File of the Berkshire Eyre, 1248*. London: Seldon Society, 1973.

Presents an edition and translation of inquiries that include sexual offenses. Thirteenth century.

52. "Concilium Elibertanum." *Patrologiae Cursus Completus, Series Latina 84.* Edited by Migne. Belgium: Brepols, 1844-55, pp. 301-310.

Contains much sexual legislation. See Samuel Laeuchli (item 422) for an analysis of this Iberian council. Fourth century.

53. Downer, L.J., trans. *Leges Henrici Primi*. Oxford: Clarendon Press, 1972.

Deals extensively with regulations on sexuality, including fornication of clergy and abortion. Twelfth century.

54. Drew, Katherine Fischer, trans. *The Burgundian Code.* Philadelphia: University of Pennsylvania Press, 1972.

Includes laws concerning rape, adultery and incest. Late fifth/ early sixth centuries.

55. ——. *The Lombard Laws*. Philadelphia: University of Pennsylvania Press, 1973.

Includes penalties for rape, fornication and incest. Seventh and eighth centuries.

56. DuPont, M.G., ed. "Le Registre de l'officialité de Cerisy, 1314-1457." *Memoirs de la société des antiquaires de Normandie. 3d ser. 10*, pp. 271-607.

Records the proceedings of the court of Cerisy in Normandy, which shows 170 convictions for sexual crimes for one decade, 1314-1323. An unusual source. Fourteenth century.

57. Gratian. *Decretum cum Glossis.* Lyon: Roussin, 1584.

Deals with many sexual issues including sodomy, homosexuality, incest, and the importance of fulfilling the marriage debt to prevent a partner's adultery. The whole is a critically important work for the study of law and sexuality. Twelfth century.

58. Gregory IX. "Decretals." *Corpus Iuris Canonici.* 2 vols. Edited by E. Friedberg. Graaz: Akademische Druck- u Verlag, 1959.

Expands earlier canon law decretals, and includes information on married sexuality. Thirteenth century.

59. Hair, Paul, ed. *Before the Bawdy Court: Selections from Church Court and Other Records...* London: Elek, 1972.

Collects court records from Scotland and New England from 1300 to 1800. Most of the selections date from later than the medieval period, but there are a few medieval ones showing punishments for adultery, fornication and lechery. Fourteenth century.

60. Helmholz, Richard H., ed. *Select Cases on Defamation to 1600.* London: Selden Society, 1985.

Presents an edition and translation of cases of slander brought in English courts. Includes imputations of adultery, bestiality, bastardy, prostitution, and venereal disease. Contains a long, informative introduction and good indexes. Thirteenth through sixteenth centuries.

61. Hincmar of Reims. "De Divortio." *Patrologiae Cursus Completus, Series Latina 126.* Edited by Migne. Belgium: Brepols, 1844-55, p. 694.

Describes in vivid detail his view of how conception takes place. Ninth century.

62. ——. "De Divortio Lotharii et Tetbergae, interrogatio xii." *Patrologiae Cursus Completus, Series Latina 125.* Edited by Migne. Belgium: Brepols, 1844-55, pp. 689:95.

Contains a discussion of those things Hincmar believed to be "against nature," including one of the earliest descriptions of lesbian activities. Ninth century.

63. ——. "Epistolae 22." *Patrologiae Cursus Completus, Series Latina 126.* Edited by Migne. Belgium: Brepols, 1844-55, pp. 137-38.

Originated a theory of marriage that required consummation by sexual intercourse to make it binding. Ninth century.

64. Isidore (pseudo). "Benedictus Levita." *Patrologiae Cursus Completus, Series Latina 97.* Edited by Migne. Belgium: Brepols, 1844-55, pp. 699-912.

Includes information about homosexuality, bestiality, and incest. Ninth century.

65. Ivo of Chartres. "Decretum." *Patrologiae Cursus Completus, Series Latina 161*. Edited by Migne. Belgium: Brepols, 1844-55, pp. 47-1022.

Offers important legislation on marital sexuality. See particularly Part 8 on marriage (including transgressions thereof), and Part 9 on incest. However, this last section is much and tediously taken with explanations of consanguinity. Late eleventh/early twelfth century.

66. ——. "Panormia." *Patrologiae Cursus Completus, Series Latina 161*. Edited by Migne. Belgium: Brepols, 1844-55, pp. 1042-344.

Develops further church law on sexuality. See particularly Book IV on concubines, Books V-VIII on marriage, including such topics as rape, impotence, and abortion. Includes denunciations of sodomy and lesbianism. Late eleventh/early twelfth century.

67. Larson, Laurence, ed. *The Earliest Norwegian Laws, Being the Gulathing Law and the Frostathing Law*. New York: Columbia University Press, 1935.

Translates two Norwegian law codes that contain legislation on a number of sexual topics, including adultery, fornication, incest, bestiality, castration, rape, and sexual insults accusing men of effeminacy or of participating as the passive partner in a homosexual encounter. Twelfth and thirteenth centuries.

68. Mansi, J.D., ed. *Sacrorum Conciliorum Nova et Amplissima Collectio,* vol 18A. Florentiae: Expensis A. Zalla, 1759.

Contains two canons (34 and 69) against homosexuality from the Council of Paris. Ninth century.

69. McNeill, J.T. and H. Gamer, eds. *Medieval Handbooks of Penance.* New York: Columbia University Press, 1938.

Presents an edition of early medieval penitentials that were a rich source of sexual legislation. For an excellent analysis of these sources, see Payer, item 468. Sixth through the twelfth centuries.

70. Meekings, C.A.F., ed. *Crown Pleas of the Wiltshire Eyre of 1249.* Devises: Wiltshire Archaeological and Natural History Society, 1961.

Includes accusations for sexual crimes. Thirteenth century.

71. Michaud-Quantin, P., ed. "Un Manuel de Confession Archaïque dans le Manuscrit Avranches 136." *Sacris Erudiri* 17 (1966), pp. 5-54.

Edits a manuscript that includes sections on fornication and "unnatural" copulation (although much of this section discusses the problem of marital consanguinity). Twelfth century.

72. Pansier, P., ed. "Histoire des Prétendues Statuts de la Reine Jeanne et de la Réglémentation de la prostitution à Avignon au moyen-âge." *Janus* 7 (1902): 1-7,64-70,143-149, 180-188.

Presents an edition and French translation of a text that regulated activities of prostitutes in Avignon. Fourteenth century.

73. Petit, Joseph, ed. *Registre des causes civiles de l'officialité épiscopale de Paris 1384-1387.* Paris: Imprimerie nationale, 1919.

Describes marriages annulled for the husbands' impotence. Fourteenth century.

74. Post, J.B., ed. "A Fifteenth-Century Customary of the Southwark Stews." *Journal of the Society of Archivists* 5:7 (April 1977): 418-28.

Edits a fifteenth-century list of customs regulating houses of prostitution in the brothel quarter of London. The customs claim to be a recording of regulations that had a long history. Fifteenth century.

75. Regino, Abbot of Prüm. *De Synodalibus Causis et Disciplinis Ecclesiasticis.* Edited by F.G.A. Wasserschleben. Graz: Akademische Druck-und Verlagsanstalt, 1904.

Collects ecclesiastical canons prohibiting various sexual activities. Early tenth century.

76. Rivers, John, trans. *The Laws of the Alamans and Bavarians.* Philadelphia: University of Pennsylvania Press, 1977.

Includes laws concerning rape, incestuous marriages, adultery, fornication, abortion, and castration. Mid-eighth century.

77. Robertson, A.J., trans. *The Laws of the Kings of England from Edmund to Henry I.* Cambridge: Cambridge University Press, 1925.

Contains a number of laws against adultery. Until the early twelfth century.

78. Riley, Henry Thomas, ed. and trans. *Liber Albus: The White Book of the City of London.* London: Richard Griffin & Co., 1861.

Offers an edition of London ordinances that regulated, among other things, prostitution. Thirteenth century.

79. Riley, Henry Thomas, ed. and trans. *Memorials of London and London Life in the XIIIth, XIVth, and XVth Centuries.* London: Longmans, Green & Co., 1868.

Collects excerpts from the archives of the City of London that illustrate various aspects of social history. This rich collection includes regulations of the brothels, a detailed trial of a procuress, warnings about intercourse with lepers, etc. Thirteenth through fifteenth centuries.

80. Scott, Samuel P., ed. *Las Siete Partidas*. Chicago: University of Chicago Press, 1931.

Contains a Spanish law code drafted for Alfonso the Wise, which gives strict penalties against those who practice homosexuality and bestiality. Thirteenth century.

81. ——. *The Visigothic Code (Forum Judicum)*. Boston: The Boston Book Co., 1910.

Translates a rich Germanic law code that includes sections of laws on adultery, incest, pederasty and sodomy. Seventh century.

82. Sharpe, R.R., ed. *Calendar of Letter-Books Preserved among the Archives of the Corporation of the City of London*. London: John Edward Francis, 1899-1920.

Provides a series of fifty volumes covering the reigns of Edward I through James II. Early volumes include proceedings of the Court of Common Council. Letter-Books A, D, F, and H regulated the activities of prostitutes between the thirteenth and fifteenth centuries.

83. Stenton, Doris Mary, ed. *Rolls of the Justices in Eyre for Lincolnshire, 1218-19*. London: Seldon Society, 1934.

Preserves trial records that include reports of rape. Thirteenth century.

84. ——. *Rolls of the Justices in Eyre for Yorkshire, 1218-19*. London: Seldon Society, 1937.

Provides trial records for such crimes as rape, although the numbers of indictments are few, because of the difficulty of proving the charge. Thirteenth century.

85. Theodore, Archbishop. "Fragmenta ex Collectoribus Canonum." *Patrologiae Cursus Completus, Series*

Latina 99. Edited by Migne. Belgium: Brepols 1844-55, pp. 966-77.

Contains a series of canons regulating various sexual activities, i.e., positions, when to abstain, fornication, rape. Seventh century.

86. Theodulf of Orleans. "Capitula ad Presbyteros Parochiae Suae." *Patrologiae Cursus Completus, Series Latina 105*. Edited by Migne. Belgium: Brepols, 1844-55, pp. 207-224.

Argues in the Second Diocesan Statute that marital sex is a venial sin. Also discusses homosexuality, incest and bestiality. Ninth century.

87. Vogel, Cyrille, ed. *Le Pecheur et la Penitence au Moyen-Age*. Paris: Les éditions du Cerf, 1969.

Offers a collection of texts in translation (to French) which show the development of penitence from early Christianity through the thirteenth century, including public penance, private penance and penitential pilgrimage. The texts are chosen to provide an excellent representative sample, and include several sections on sexual sins, including lesbianism (in the penitentials of Bede and Burchard) which is rare to find, bestiality, sodomy, fornication, prostitution and love sorcery. The book also provides a solid introduction and a complete bibliography.

88. ——. *Les 'Libri Paenitentiales.' Typologie des sources du moyen âge occidental 27*. Turnhout: Brepols, 1978.

Contains legislation on sexual acts. See Payer, item 468 for an analysis of this important source. Sixth through the twelfth century.

89. Weinbaum, Martin, ed. *The London Eyre of 1276*. London: Seldon Society, 1976.

Contains trial records that include rape accounts. Thirteenth century.

90. Werminghoff, A., ed. "Concilia aevi Karolini." *Monumenta Germaniae Historica, Legum Sectio III,* vol. 2. Hanover: Hahn, 1906-08, p. 50.

Ninth century.

91. Woodbine, G.E.,ed. *Four Thirteenth Century Law Tracts*. New Haven: Yale University Press, 1912.

Reproduces legal tracts that include discussions on rape. Thirteenth century.

PRIMARY SOURCES

LITERATURE

Literary sources often favor love (and consequently sex) as a theme, and medieval literature is no exception. The sources are very rich, but in their richness there is ambiguity. I had a difficult time choosing among those works that are "courtly" and those that are "sexual," since, particularly in literature, there are no sharp lines of distinction. For example, *The Lais of Marie de France* (item 141) are mostly courtly tales, but they do include some references to castration and homosexuality, so I have included them here.

The selections below include material that ranges from poetry (latin and vernacular) and romances, to sagas, dramas, and fabliaux. The fabliaux are the richest source of sexually explicit material; most of the 160 surviving fabliaux revolve around situations of actual or attempted fornication. These tales influenced future collections, like those of Boccaccio and Chaucer. (Six and a half of Chaucer's tales, the bawdiest, were based on fabliaux). I have included several collections that contain sexually explicit or scatological tales. For a complete listing of fabliaux bibliography, see Per Nykrog (item 458) or R. Eichmann and J. Duval (item 115).

92. Alexander, Michael, ed. *The Earliest English Poems.* Berkeley: University of California Press, 1970.

Includes poems and riddles. For information about sexuality, see especially the riddles, which are full of witty sexual double entendres (for example, numbers 25 and 44) and also contain one of the earliest direct references to female masturbation (riddle #12). Early eighth century.

93. Ancona, Alessandro, ed., *Leggenda di Vergogna.* Bologna: Editrice Forni, 1967.

Provides an edition of a medieval Italian work that describes father/daughter incest. Thirteenth century.

94. Andreas Capellanus. *The Art of Courtly Love.* Edited by John Jay Parry. New York: Frederick Ungar Publishing Co., 1959.

Contains what is traditionally considered the handbook description of courtly love. There are enough elements of sexuality in it (for example, his advocacy of rape of peasant girls) to make it valuable as a guide to attitudes and practice of sexuality. Twelfth century.

95. Bellows, Henry Adams, trans. *The Poetic Edda.* New York: Biblo and Tannen, 1969.

Portrays (particularly in "Lokasenna") classically Icelandic sexual insults, accusing a woman of unbridled lust, incest, and accusing a man of effeminacy, bearing children and allowing his mouth to be used as a "privy." Unfortunately, the translation presented here, while easily accessible, does not present the material in the same vigorous language as the original. Twelfth century.

96. Blodgett, E.D. and R. A. Swanson, trans. *The Love Songs of the Carmina Burana.* New York: Garland Publishing, Inc., 1987.

Translates love songs found in the Carmina Burana collection. Most of the poems are abstract love lyrics as might be found in courtly love collections, but many describe vivid sexual encounters that express attitudes toward sexuality. See, for examples, poems 72, 84, and 158 for descriptions of rape; poems 83 and 185 for seductions; poem 121 for sadism; and poem 65 for an implication of homosexual love. Contains a full bibliography and complete textual notes. Late twelfth, early thirteenth century.

97. Blonquist, Lawrence, trans. *L'Art D'Amours.* New York: Garland Publishing, Inc., 1987.

Presents an accessible translation of a French rendition of Ovid's *Art of Love.* Fourteenth century.

98. Boccaccio, Giovanni. *The Decameron.* Translated by G.H. McWilliam. New York: Penguin, 1972.

Recounts one hundred tales, many of which include accounts of fornication and adultery. Tale six from the Fifth Day has a homosexual theme, and tale ten from the Third Day has frequently been singled out for censorship but these are by no means the only examples of stories with sexual themes. Fourteenth century.

99. Bogin, Meg. *The Women Troubadours.* New York: Norton, 1980.

Includes a poem by Bieiris de Romans that seems to praise lesbian love. Early thirteenth century.

100. Bologna, Corrado, ed. *Liber Monstrorum de Diversis Generibus: Libro delle Miraboli Difformita.* Milan: Bompiani, 1977.

Contains descriptions of various monsters, and some include references to homosexuality. Twelfth century.

101. Brians, Paul. *Bawdy Tales from the Courts of Medieval France.* New York: Harper Torchbooks, 1973.

Provides a prose translation of ten fabliaux that contain themes of fornication, adultery and trickery. The prose does not adequately reproduce the poetic original. Thirteenth century.

102. Brunner, Karl, ed. *Seven Sages of Rome.* London: Oxford University Press, 1933.

Tells a story of a prince who is accused of incest with one of his father's wives. He is defended by seven wise men who tell stories of infidelities and women's deviousness. Includes a story of transvestism. There are many editions of this work in many languages, see John Keller (item 136) for a translation of the Spanish version and a good discussion of the tradition of the tales. Late twelfth or early thirteenth century.

103. Chaucer, Geoffrey. *The Canterbury Tales.* Translated by Nevill Coghill. New York: Penguin, 1982.

Collects a number of tales, many of which have sexual themes. The tales most commonly cited as illuminating attitudes on sexuality are the Miller's, Reeves', Merchant's, and Parson's tales, but the Prologue and other transition passages are also revealing. Fourteenth Century.

104. ——. *The Parlement of Foulys.* Edited by D.S. Brewer. London: Thomas Nelson, Ltd., 1960.

Relates a dream in which the God Priapus is decorated with garlands, and birds debate about love. Fourteenth century.

105. Chrétien de Troyes. *Arthurian Romances.* Translated by W.W. Comfort. London: J.M. Dent & Sons, Ltd., 1970.

Presents an edition of four of Chrétien's romances, *Erec et Enide, Cligès, Yvain et Lancelot*. They present Chrétien's ambivalent attitude toward sex, including his fear that it is a socially disruptive force. Within these tales of quests and adventures are some descriptions of sexual encounters. Notable is the description of Enide's wedding night when she loses her virginity. Twelfth century.

* Coleman, Janet, ed. and trans. "*The Owl and the Nightingale* and Papal Theories of Marriage." Cited below as item 588.

Includes the text and translation of the poem. Late twelfth or early thirteenth century.

106. Conti, Gianfranco, ed. *Poeti del Duecento,* vol. 1. Milan-Napoli: Ricciardi, 1960.

Includes a Sicilian poem by Cielo D'Alcamo, *Contrasto*, which has a rare reference to necrophilia. Mid-thirteenth century.

107. Cormier, Raymond, ed., *Three Ovidian Tales of Love*. New York: Garland Publishing, Inc., 1986.

Presents a translation of three Anglo-Norman stories that had been based on Ovid. The first two tales present tragic, unconsummated love stories in the tradition of chivalric romances. The third tale, that of "Philomena et Procne" by Chrétien de Troyes, is different. This is a dark story of obsessive passion which leads to rape, mutilation, infanticide and cannibalism, which lets the author once again present his suspicion of the canon of love. Twelfth century.

108. Crow, Joan, ed. *Les Quinze Joyes de Mariage*. Oxford: Basil Blackwell, 1969.

Edits an Old French satire on the evils of the married state. Considered a misogynist tract for its listing of the evils of women, among them a propensity for adultery. Late fourteenth century.

* Daniel, Arnaut. "The Song of Nail and Uncle: Arnaut Daniel's Sestina 'Lo fem voler q'el cor m'intra.'" Edited by Charles Jernigan. Cited below as item 660.

Includes an edition and translation of the sestina within an excellent analysis of the poem. Twelfth century.

109. De Montaiglon, A., *et al.*, eds. *Recueil Général et Complet des Fabliaux des XIIIe et XIVe Siècles* (6 vols.) Paris: 1872-90.

Edits short bawdy tales. While this edition is fairly inaccessible, it remains the most complete record of the fabliaux. Thirteenth and fourteenth century.

110. Diner, Judith Bruskin, trans. *Les Cent Nouvelles Nouvelles*. New York: Garland Publishing, Inc., 1990.

Collects and translates one hundred French prose tales, many of which are quite bawdy. Fifteenth century.

111. Doutrepont, August, ed. *La Clef D'Amors.* Halle: M. Niemeyer, 1890.

Presents an old French rendition of Ovid's *Ars Amatoria*, which follows Ovid, yet brings its own particular modification to the text. Includes descriptions of seduction and advocacy of rape. A popular and influential work. See Shapiro (Item 163) for a translation of some excerpts.

112. Dronke, Peter, ed. *Medieval Latin and the Rise of European Love-Lyric , 2 vol.* Oxford: Clarendon Press, 1968.

Studies courtly love with Peter Dronke's impeccable scholarship. Does not deal explicitly with sexuality, but I include it here because volume II contains editions and translations of previously unpublished love lyrics. Most of them treat love in the abstract, but a few are quite remarkable in their direct treatment of seduction, incest, and an unusual piece describing pedophilia.

113. Drouart La Vache. *Li Livres d'Amours.* Edited by Robert Bossuat. Paris: Librairie Ancienne Honore Cham., 1926.

Translates into old French the *De Amore* of Andreas Capellanus, and creates a source that sheds further light on sexuality by the liberties he takes with Andreas' text. For an excellent analysis of this source, see Jacquart and Thomasset (item 408). See Shapiro (item 163) for a translation. Thirteenth century.

114. Eichmann, R., ed. *Cuckolds, Clerics and Countrymen: Medieval French Fabliaux.* Fayetteville: University of Arkansas Press, 1982.

Presents editions and verse translations of ten fabliaux, which contain explicitly sexual material. Thirteenth century.

115. Eichmann, R. and J. DuVal, eds. *The French Fabliau, B.N.MS. 837,* 2 vols. New York: Garland Publishing, Inc., 1984.

Contains forty fabliaux selected from one manuscript. Presents parallel text of edition with translation. The translations are easy to read, and preserve the spirit of the original. Several of these tales contain the kind of detail that is useful in a study of sexuality. See, for example, "Boivin" for seduction, "Jouglet" for vivid scatology, "Aloul" for detailed, if improbable descriptions of intercourse. Thirteenth century.

116. Élie, Maître. *Maître Élie Überarbeitung der ältesten franzosischen Übertragung von Ovid's Ars Amatoria.* Marburg: N.G. Elwert, 1886.

Presents an old French adaptation of Ovid's *Ars Amatoria.* Maître Élie reset the work in Paris, and added contemporary descriptions of Parisian erotic life. See Shapiro (item 163) for a translation of some excerpts. Thirteenth century.

117. Elliott, Alison Goddard, trans. "The Facetus: Or The Art of Courtly Living." *Allegorica,* 2 (1977), 27-57.

Offers a manual of love and seduction. Contains recommendations for seduction, kissing, touching, and finally rape if the maiden remains reluctant. Twelfth century.

118. ——. *Seven Medieval Latin Comedies.* New York: Garland Publishing, Inc., 1984.

Includes comedies that vividly describe seduction, passion and rape within stories of love and infidelity drawn from Ovid, Terence and Plautus. Twelfth century.

119. *Esclarmonde, Clarisse et Florent, Yde et Olive - Drei Fortsetzungen der Chanson von Huon de Bordeaux, nach der einzigen Turiner Handschrift zum ersten Mal veröffentlicht. Ausgaben v. Abhandlungen aus dem Gebiete der Romanischen Philologie* 83. Edited by Max Schweigel. Marburg: N.G. Elwert'sche Verlagsbuchhandlung, 1889.

Contains the romance of *Yde et Olive* in which the heroine travels in men's clothing to escape her father's incestuous advances, marries a woman, then is miraculously transformed into a man. Thirteenth century.

120. "Estoire de Merlin." *The Vulgate Version of Arthurian Romances*. Edited from Manuscripts in the British Museum, vol 3. Edited by H. Oskar Sommer. Washington: The Carnegie Institute, 1910.

Tells a complex story of transvestism. Thirteenth century.

121. Fell, Christine, trans. *Egil's Saga*. Toronto: University of Toronto Press, 1975.

Contains short references to impotence as the final tragedy of a warrior in his old age as his strength too wanes. Twelfth century.

122. Finch, R.G., trans. *The Saga of the Volsungs.* London: Nelson, 1965.

Contains an account of an incestuous relationship between brother and sister. Thirteenth century.

123. García Gómez, E., trans. *El Libre de las Banderas de los Campeones*. Madrid: Imprenta de la Vuida de E. Maestre, 1942.

Provides an anthology of Arabic poetry of al-Andalus in Spain. Contains some poems that praise the love of boys.

124. Geoffroy de la Tour. *The Book of the Knight of La Tour-Landry.* Translated by Thomas Wright. New York: Greenwood Press, 1969.

Gathers stories from scripture, saints' lives, fabliaux and other sources to write a book for his three daughters' education. To exhort his daughters to chastity and virtue, the knight included tales of lechery, fornication, and intercourse on an altar. Fourteenth century.

125. Guiart. "L'Art D'Amor." *Zeitschrift für Romanische Philologie* 45 (1924): 66-80, 181-87.

Provides an edition of a French poem on the art of love. It is mostly a repudiation of earthly love, but seduction is described graphically as rape. See Shapiro (item 163) for a translation. Thirteenth century.

126. Guillame de Lorris and Jean de Meun. *Roman de La Rose.* Translated by C. Dahlberg. Princeton: Princeton University Press, 1971.

Presents an allegory that for three hundred years remained immensely popular. Within the allegory/dream, the lover strives for and finally attains a Rose. It has generated much controversy on the view of love portrayed as well as on its literary themes. The scholarship so far has not dealt fully with the sexual attitudes revealed in the work. For full bibliographies refer to Luria, Poirion, and Jung (items 440, 474, 663). Thirteenth century.

127. Harrison, Robert, trans. *Gallic Salt.* Berkeley: University of California Press, 1974.

Offers an English translation of eighteen French fabliaux, many of which contain sexually explicit material. See especially, "*Du Chevelier Qui fit les Cons Parler.*" Thirteenth century.

128. Heldris de Cornuälle. *Le Roman de Silence.* Edited by Lewis Thorpe. Cambridge: Heffer, 1972.

Tells a story of a woman who dresses as a man to gain her inheritance. Thirteenth century.

129. Hellman, R. and R. O'Gorman. *Fabliaux: Ribald Tales from the Old French*. New York: Crowell, 1965.

Offers a prose translation of twenty-two French fabliaux, which include tales of infidelity, fornication, and scatology which are characteristic of the genre. The prose translation does not do justice to the original works. Thirteenth century.

130. Hicks, Eric, ed. *Le débat sur le Roman de la Rose.* Paris: H. Champion, 1977.

Records a debate on the merits and morality of the *Roman de la Rose*, and reveals changing and conflicting attitudes toward sexuality. Early fifteenth century.

131. Hilary the Englishman. *Hilarii versus et ludi.* Edited by John Bernard Fuller. New York: Holt, 1929.

Includes poetry praising homosexual love. Twelfth century.

132. Hilka, Alfons and Otto Schumann, eds. *Carmina Burana*. Heidelberg: Carl Winter's Universitätsbuchhandlung, 1930-41.

Presents a collection of satiric poetry that includes sexual material. See Blodgett (item 96) for a translation of the body of love songs included in this collection. Late twelfth and thirteenth centuries.

133. Hroswitha. *The Plays of Roswitha.* Translated by Christopher St. John. New York: Benjamin Blom, 1923.

Includes the play, "Paphnutius," which describes the conversion of the prostitute, Thaïs.

134. Johnston, George, trans. *The Saga of Gisli*. Toronto: University of Toronto Press, 1963.

Describes an incident in which a wooden effigy of two men engaged in a homosexual act is made to insult the passive party depicted. This example shows one way sexual acts were used as expressions of power in Scandinavian society. Twelfth century.

135. Jones, Lowanne E., trans. *The "Cort d'Amour": A Thirteenth-Century Allegorical Art of Love.* Chapel Hill, NC: University of North Carolina Press, 1977.

Depicts a vivid advocacy of rape (lines 574-584). The translator unconvincingly argues that rape was not really intended. Thirteenth century.

136. Keller, John Esten, trans. *The Book of the Wiles of Women.* Chapel Hill: University of North Carolina Press, 1956.

Translates this Spanish version of *The Seven Sages* (item 102). Includes tales of adultery and fornication. This translation has a brief but excellent introduction, which describes the tradition of the transmission of these tales. The story was translated into Arabic in the eighth century, then from Arabic to Spanish in the thirteenth century.

137. Laurent. *The Book of Vices and Virtues: A Fourteenth-Century English Translation of the* Somme le Roi. Edited by W. Nelson Francis. London: Oxford University Press, 1942.

Compare with item 138, edited by Brunni. Thirteenth century.

138. Lorenzo d'Orléans. *Libru di li Vitii et di li Virtuti,* 3 vols. Edited by Francesco Bruni. Palermo: Centro di Studi Filologici e linguistici Siciliani, 1973.

Offers a version of the *Somme le Roi* of Lorenzo d'Orléans that was written ca. 1279. The information on sexuality in the text is limited, but the comments on adultery and fornication do yield some insights into sexual attitudes. This edition contains extensive introduction and commentary, as well as a complete index. Early fourteenth-century version of a thirteenth-century text.

139. Magnusson, M. and Hermann Palsson, trans. *Laxdaela Saga*. Harmondsworth: Penguin, 1969.

Contains an example of a woman dressing in men's clothing and arming herself to avenge a wrong. Thirteenth century.

140. ——. *Njal's Saga.* New York: Penguin, 1986.

Tells of a man who had sex with Queen Gunnhild the Queen Mother of Norway. When he was ready to go home to marry, she put a spell on him that his erection would be too large to permit him to consummate a marriage. This sets up a series of events that leads to disaster. Thirteenth century.

141. Marie de France. *The Lais of Marie de France.* Translated by R. Hanning and J. Ferrante. Durham, NC: Labyrinth Press, 1978.

Offers an excellent translation of the twelve "lais" (short romances). The lais lie somewhere between the bawdy fabliaux and the more abstract, courtly romances as far as their references to sexuality. There is not a lot of information directly on sex, but the occasional references to castration (in "Guigemar") and homosexuality (in "Lanval") shed light on sexual attitudes. Late twelfth century.

142. Matthew of Vendôme. "Ars Versificatoria." *Les Arts Poétiques du XIIe et du XIIIe siècle.* Edited by E. Faral. Paris: H. Champion, 1962, pp. 106-93.

Contains a number of sexually explicit references. Particularly useful for developing Matthew's attitudes toward sexuality. Late twelfth century.

143. ———. "Milo." *La Comédie Latine en France au XIIe Siècle,* vol 1. Edited by Marcel Abraham. Paris: Société d'édition "Les Belles-lettres," 1931, pp. 155-77.

Recounts a tale of adultery. Late twelfth century.

144. McGrew, Julia H. trans. *Sturlunga Saga*. New York: Twayne Publishers, Inc., 1970.

Describes Icelandic society in the thirteenth century, during which morals were said to have declined. This saga contains numerous references to sexual behavior outside marriage, and may shed light on sexual attitudes in Iceland during this time. Ritual castration as defeat of an enemy, shown in Sturla Portharson's *Islendinga Saga,* is also included in this collection. Thirteenth century.

145. Monroe, James, trans. *Hispano-Arab Poetry*. Berkeley: University of California Press, 1974.

Collects Arabic poetry of al-Andalus in Spain. Readable translations including a number that refer to homosexual love. Many of the more scatological poems have been omitted, however. A fuller collection may be found in Emilio Garcia Gomez's work on the subject (item 123).

146. Nelson, Venetia, ed. *A Myrour to Lewd Men and Wymmen*. Heidelberg: Carl Winter, 1981.

Deals with the sin of lechery, and in warning against this sin, mentions some practices of foreplay and describes the development of lust. This is a middle English edition of a late fourteenth century prose version of the *Speculum Vitae*, a northern English poem of the late fourteenth century. Fifteenth-century tract.

147. Nigel de Longchamps. *Speculum Stultorum*. Edited by J.H. Mozley and R.R. Raymo. Berkely: University of California Press, 1960.

Presents a poetic satire of monks, accusing them of moral laxity. See item 172 for another edition. Late twelfth century.

148. Nykl, Alois Richard, trans. *Hispano-Arab Poetry and its Relations with the Old Provencal Troubadours*. Baltimore: J.H. Furst Co., 1946.

Contains a number of poems of homosexual love, but some of the more explicit poems of this type were excluded from the collection. A fuller treatment may be found in Emilio Garcia Gomez's anthology (item 123).

149. Orson de Beauvois. *Orson de Beauvois*. Edited by G. Paris. Paris: S.A.T.F., 1899.

Describes the use of an herb that would render an unwanted lover impotent. Twelfth century.

150. Paden, William D., trans. *The Medieval Pastourelle*. New York: Garland Publishing, Inc., 1987.

Provides a complete edition and translation of medieval pastourelles. The defining elements of this poetry include the attempted seduction of a peasant girl by a young nobleman. The poetry is full of accounts of rape as well as seduction and rejection. This work has a particularly rich bibliography.

151. Palsson, Hermann, trans. *Hrafnkel's Saga and other Icelandic Stories.* Harmondsworth: Penguin, 1976.

Contains accusations of homosexuality, effeminacy, and bestiality. See especially "*Olkofra Thattr.*" Late thirteenth/early fourteenth century.

152. Pérès, Henri, trans. *La Poésie Andalouse en Arabe Classique au XIe siècle*. Paris: Adrien-Maisonneuve, 1953.

Translates Spanish Arabic poetry which contains fairly explicit references to eroticism, both heterosexual and homosexual. Eleventh century.

153. Peter of Blois. *Une Traité de l'Amours du XIIe Siècle.* Edited by M.M. Davie. Paris: E. de Boccard, 1932.

Presents an edition and French translation of a mystical tract that extols love of soul with God, and the joys of loving friendship. Also discusses carnal love to point up the contrast, thus providing insight into his views on sexuality. Twelfth century.

154. Philippe de Beaumanoir. "La Manekine." *Oeuvres Poétiques de Beaumanoir,* vol. 1. Edited by Hermann Suchier. Paris: Firmin Didot, 1884.

Tells a tale in which the theme is father/daughter incest and transvestism. Thirteenth century.

155. ——. *Philippe de Beaumanoir, La Manekine: Roman du XIIIe Siècle.* Translated by C. Marchello-Nizia. Paris: Stock, 1980.

Provides a French translation of "La Manekine" (item 154). Includes an analytic essay listed below as item 703). Thirteenth century.

156. Richard de Fournival. *Mittelalteinische Studien und Texte 2.* Leiden: Brill, 1967.

Relates a tale (*De Vetula*) of a young man who makes love to a beautiful woman only to find he had actually been making love to the elderly bawd. Thirteenth century.

157. Rickard, Peter, *et al.*, trans. *Medieval Comic Tales*. Totowa, NJ: Rowman & Littlefield, 1973.

Collects and translates short tales that include themes of adultery, fornication, castration, and the debilitating effects of intercourse. Includes French, Spanish, English, Italian, German, Dutch, and Latin stories that range from the eleventh to the fifteenth centuries.

158. Robert de Blois. "Chastoiement des Dames." *Robert de Blois, son Oeuvre Didactique et Narrative*. Edited by John H. Fox. Paris: Nizet, 1950.

Offers severe moralistic advice to women, which includes explicit suggestions such as urging women to keep their tunics closed so men cannot fondle their breasts. See Shapiro (item 163) for a translation. Thirteenth century.

* Roth, Norman, trans. "Satire and Debate in Two Famous Medieval Poems from al-Andalus." Cited below as item 761.

Provides translations of two poems by the Hebrew poets, Yosef Ibn Hasday and Samuel Ibn Nagrillah. Eleventh century.

159. Roy, Bruno, ed. *Devinettes Françaises du Moyen Age*. Montreal: Bellarmin, 1977.

Collects medieval French riddles and includes a number of scatological ones and others that have sexual double-entendres.

160. Rudolf von Schlettstadt. *Rudolf von Schlettstadt: Historiae Memorabiles. Zur Dominikanerliteratur und Kulturgeschichte des 13. Jahrhunderts*. Edited by E. Kleinschmidt. Cologne-Vienna: 1974.

Collects a number of exemplary tales, many of which have sexual themes, including one in which a peasant has intercourse with his menstruating wife and she conceives a monster. Thirteenth century.

161. Ruiz, Juan. *The Book of Good Love.* Translated by E.K. Kane. Chapel Hill, NC: University of North Carolina Press, 1968.

Contains a good deal of information on sexuality that has not yet been systematically analyzed. The story and the parables and songs contained within it include folk wisdom about sex, (for example, it saps a youth's strength), give instruction on seduction, describe features considered sexually attractive, and yield creative double-entendres. Includes the rape scene taken from the popular medieval play, Pamphilus. This translation contains a good introductory essay by John E. Keller, and an extensive bibliography on the literary analysis of the source. Fourteenth century.

162. Salverda de Grave, J.-J., ed. *Le Roman d'Eneas,* 2 vols. Paris: C.F.M.A., 1964-68.

Contains references to homosexuality. Twelfth century.

163. Shapiro, Norman, trans. *The Comedy of Eros: Medieval French Guides to the Art of Love.* Urbana: University of Illinois Press, 1971.

Translates into English a sample of vernacular literature which followed Ovid in offering instruction on the art of love. Includes works by Maître Élie, Guiart, Robert of Blois, Drouart la Vache, Richard de Fournival and others. This is a fine translation of relatively inaccessible materials. Thirteenth century.

164. Silagi, Gabriel, ed. "Ein Pedantscher Liebesbrief aus dem 14. Jahrhundert." *Archiv für Kulturgeschichte* 51 (1969): 234-62.

Provides an edition of a tract on love from Bavaria, with a summary of the text in German. Fourteenth century.

165. Sinclair, K.V., ed. *Tristan de Nanteuil, Chanson de Geste Inédite.* Assen: Van Gorcum and Comp., 1971.

Tells of a woman dressed as a man whose gender is miraculously changed. Fourteenth century.

166. Snorri Sturluson. *Heimskringla: History of the Kings of Norway.* Translated by L.M. Hollander. Austin, TX: University of Texas Press, 1964.

Describes the castrating of King Magnus in 1135. It was done to remove his power symbolically so that he could never again be king. Reveals the repeated Scandinavian association between masculinity, sexuality and power. Twelfth century.

167. Stehling, Thomas, trans. *Medieval Latin Poems of Male Love and Friendship.* New York: Garland Publishing, Inc., 1984.

Offers texts and translations from more than thirty medieval poets on the subject of male love and friendship. It includes materials both favorable and unfavorable to homosexual relationships. The book is arranged chronologically, beginning with the late classical period and ending with a collection of anonymous works from the twelfth century and later. It is a diverse and fascinating collection, but the work is marred by translation problems. Before twelfth century.

168. Swan, Charles, trans. *Gesta Romanorum,* 2 vols. Edited by Thomas Wright. New York: J.W. Bouton, 1871.

Translates short tales from a British manuscript. These tales are exempla of moral conduct, and as such, reveal much about sexuality. See, for examples, "Of Inordinate Love" for incest; "Of the Execrable Devices of Old Women" for adultery; "Of a Sinful and Leprous Soul" for associations of sexuality with leprosy. Fourteenth century.

169. Villon, François. *The Poems of François Villon.* Translated by Galway Kinnell. London: University Press of New England, 1977.

Includes a translation of Villon's "Testament," which includes many references to sexuality, and sexual double entendres. Within this poem is the ballad to Fat Margot, a prostitute in a brothel. Fifteenth century.

170. von der Hagen, Friederich Heinrich, ed. "Der Vrouwen Turnei." *Gesamtabenteuer: Hundert altdeutsche Erzählungen.* vol. 1. Darmstadt: Wissenschaftliche Buchgesellschaft, 1961, pp. 371-82.

Relates a German tale in which a community of women dress as men in order to joust. Not only does the story describe transvestism, but it ends with an elaborate sexual play on words. Thirteenth century.

171. Wright, Thomas, ed. *Anecdota Literaria.* London: John Russell Smith, 1844.

Collects a number of short poems in English, Latin, and French from England. They were chosen to illustrate medieval life and manners, and include fabliaux (including two precursors of Chaucer's "Miller's Tale"), Goliardic poetry and other miscellany. Thirteenth century.

172. ———. *Anglo-Latin Satirical Poets and Epigrammatists of the Twelfth Century.* London: Longman & Co., 1872.

Contains an edition of the *Speculum Stultorum*, a satire on monastic vice (see item 147 for another edition), and the long satiric poem, *Architrenius,* by John de Hauteville, which discusses the miseries and vices of humanity, and Alan of Lille's *De Planctu Naturae* (see item 179). Contains riddles and other shorter satirical works. Twelfth century.

173. Zapperi, R. *L'Homme Enceint*. Paris: Presses Universitaires Françaises, 1983.

Recounts a fourteenth-century humorous story of a man who believed he could get pregnant by having intercourse in the woman superior position.

PRIMARY SOURCES

RELIGION

Since the documents that survived from the Middle Ages did so mostly because of ecclesiastical care, in some ways this category consists of all those things that did not obviously belong in one of the other chapters. I have included saints' lives, religious tracts, letters, sermons, episcopal visitation records, and inquisition registers. Due to medieval interests and university structures, there is much overlap between these sources and those listed under science, so these two chapters should be consulted jointly. The principal characteristic of the religious sources is their didactic purpose. Sexual information is not included as anecdotes (as in the historical sources), nor dispassionately (as in the scientific ones), but for morally uplifting reasons. Therefore, use of these sources poses a number of methodological problems. For example, can we assume people were actually doing what churchman were preaching against, or did sermons reflect the individual rather than the society? However, these and similar questions are only cautionary, and do not prevent these works from being useful sources of information on sexual attitudes and practices. The abundance of medieval religious sources keeps this list from being comprehensive, and there is much manuscript material that has not yet been analyzed.

174. Abelard, Peter. "Expositio of Romans." *Patrologiae Cursus Completus, Series Latina 178*. Edited by Migne. Belgium: Brepols, 1844-55. p. 888.

Contains Abelard's discussion of concupiscence as sin. See Abelard (item 175) for a more sophisticated development of his thought on this matter. Twelfth century.

175. ——. *Ethica*. Translated by D.A. Luscombe. Oxford: Clarendon Press, 1971.

Contains Abelard's argument that carnal pleasure was natural, thus not intrinsically evil. Twelfth century.

176. "Acta S. Godelivas." *Analecta Bollandiana* 44 (1926): 102-137.

Includes the accusation of lesbian activity within a story of domestic brutality. Eleventh century.

177. Aelred of Rievaulx. "Speculum Caritatis." *Aelredi Rievallensis opera omnia* (Corpus Christianorum) Edited by A. Hoste and H. Talbot. Turnhout: Brepols, 1970.

Discusses friendship with homosexual connotations. Also see, Aelred, *On Spiritual Friendship* (item 178). Twelfth century.

178. ——. *Spiritual Friendship*. (Cistercian Fathers Series, no. 5) Translated by Mary Laker. Kalamazoo, MI: Cistercian Publications, 1974.

Discusses monastic friendship, and has been used as evidence for homosexual relations. There is, of course, controversy as to how literally this work should be interpreted. I am inclined to agree that the content is sufficiently erotic to suggest physical homosexuality. See also Aelred's *Mirror of Charity* (item 177) for similar expressions. Twelfth century.

179. Alan of Lille. *The Plaint of Nature.* Translated by James J. Sheridan. Toronto: Pontifical Institute, 1980.

Translates the classic and much quoted attack of homosexuality. Twelfth century.

180. Anselm, Archbishop of Canterbury. "De nuptiis consanguineorum." *Patrologiae Cursus Completus, Series Latina 158*. Edited by Migne. Belgium: Brepols, 1844-55, pp. 557-560.

Deals mainly with marriage, but it contains some comments on intercourse. Eleventh century.

181. ——. "De Presbyteris concubinaniis seu offendiculum clericorum." *Patrologiae Cursus Completus, Series Latina 158*. Edited by Migne. Belgium: Brepols, 1844-55, pp. 555-556.

Criticizes clerical lust. Eleventh century.

182. Augustine. *Against Julian.* Translated by M. Schumacher. New York: Fathers of the Church, 1957.

Translates a fascinating work written in response to Pelagian accusations of Manichaeanism in which Augustine explains most fully his theories of sexuality and original sin. Early fifth century.

183. Bannister, H.E. "Visitation Returns of the Diocese of Hereford, 1397." *English Historical Review* 44 (1929), 279-89.

Presents an edition of the visitation record for that year which includes complaints of incest and adultery. Fourteenth century.

184. Basil. *On the Renunciation of the World.* Translated by M. Monica Wagner. New York: Fathers of the Church, Inc., 1950.

Describes the way a prostitute might seduce someone dedicated to chastity, using words, looks, and food to weaken a monk's resolve.

185. Bede. *Bede's Ecclesiastical History of the English People.* Translated by B. Colgrave and R.A.B. Mynors. Oxford: Clarendon Press, 1969.

Includes the letter of Gregory the Great to Augustine of Canterbury that articulates Gregory's view on sexuality, including whether nocturnal emissions are sinful, and whether menstruation is polluting. See item 199 for an edition of the same letter. Late seventh/ early eighth century.

186. Bernard of Clairveaux. "Epistola 174." *Patrologiae Cursus Completus, Series Latina 182*. Edited by Migne. Belgium: Brepols, 1844-55, p. 335.

Argues against the Immaculate Conception, saying there has to be sin with carnal lust, and the Holy Spirit could not have anything to do with sin. Twelfth century.

187. Bernardo of Siena. *La Prediche Volgari*. Edited by P. Bargellini. Milan: Rizzoli, 1936.

Collects sermons in which a monk preaches against sodomy and other sexual sins. Fifteenth century.

188. Caesarius of Arles. "Sermon 447." *Corpus Christianorum, Series Latina* 103. Edited by G. Morin. Turnhout: Brepols, 1953, p. 199.

Claims that those who have intercourse on religious days of abstinence or when women were menstruating would beget lepers and epileptics. Early sixth century.

189. Caesarius of Heisterbach. *Dialogue of Miracles*, 2 vols. Translated by H. von E. Scott and C.C. Swinton Bland. London: George Routledge & Sons, Ltd., 1929.

Provides a lively translation of a dialogue between a monk and a novice on faith and monastic life that includes many anecdotes on sin, temptation, and sexuality (including sodomy, transvestism and leprosy). Offers examples of priests and monks falling into fornication, including the story of a priest whose physician told him he needed to have intercourse with a woman or die. The priest tried the cure and died anyway. Caesarius also provides a great deal of information on demons, including demon intercourse. He discusses incubi and their capacity to gather "wasted seed" to impregnate women, and describes people who died from embracing demons. Readers should note this translation uses the archaic meaning of "luxury" to mean lust. Early thirteenth century.

190. Cassian, John. "Concerning the Spirit of Fornication, Institutes of the Coenobia, ch. 6." *Corpus Scriptorum Ecclesiasticorum Latinorum,* 17. Edited by Michael Pelschenig. Prague: F. Tempsky, 1888, pp. 113-127.

Discusses the nature of fornication and how monks might fight against the temptations of lust. Early fifth century.

191. ———. "Conferences." *Corpus Scriptorum Ecclesiasticorum Latinorum.* Edited by Michael Petschenig. Vindobonae: G. Geroldi Filium, 1886.

Discusses the nature of lust and how to fight against it and its expression in nocturnal emissions. Also considers the nature of eunuchs. See particularly chapters 4, 5, 12, and 22. Early fifth century.

192. Clement. "Stromateis, III, 3, On Marriage." *Alexandrian Christianity.* Edited by J.F.L. Oulton and H. Chadwick. Philadelphia: Westminster Press, 1954, pp. 40-92.

Presents an argument in favor of marriage and marital intercourse. Includes comments on contraception, aphrodisiacs, prostitutes and homosexuals. Second century.

193. "Cod. Sign. n. 212 (al. 178 2/c)." *Analecta Bollandiana* 8 (1889): 188-91.

Includes within a list of the miracles of the Virgin Mary one in which she separates a couple whose genitals remained joined after intercourse.

194. Epiphanius. "Panarion, 2.25." *Die Grieschischen Schriftsteller der ersten drei Jahrhunderte.* Edited by K. Holl. Leipzig: J.C. Hinrichs, 1915, pp. 275-300.

Describes purported orgies of the "Barbelotites," an early Christian dualist sect. Fourth century.

195. Foulques of Deuil. "Epistola ad Abaelardum." *Patrologiae Cursus Completus, Series Latina 178*. Edited by Migne. Belgium: Brepols, 1844-55.

Discusses Abelard's life and comments on his sins and downfall, including his love affair with Héloïse. Twelfth century.

196. Fournier, Jacques. *Le Registre d'Inquisition de Jacques Fournier,* eveque de Pamiers (1318-1325) 3 vols. Edited by E. Duvernoy. Toulouse: Privat, 1965.

Edits the inquisitorial record of Jacques de Fournier which includes accounts of prostitution, sodomy and forced femoral intercourse. Emmanuel LeRoy Ladurie (item 421) created a remarkable analysis of this source. Fourteenth century.

197. Fulgentius of Ruspe. *Sancti Fulgentii Episcopi Ruspenses Opera.* Corpus Christianorum series latina 191. Edited by J. Fraipont. Turnhout: Brepols, 1968.

Ranks marital relations as venial sins in letter 1. Fifth century.

198. Gilles de Corbeil. *Essai sur la Société Médicale et Religieuse au XIIe Siècle.* Edited by Camille Vieillard. Paris: H. Champion, 1909.

Contains an edition of "*Hierapigra Galeni*," which describes and condemns homosexual acts among clergy. Twelfth century.

199. Gregory the Great. "Epistola 11." *Patrologiae Cursus Completus, Series Latina 77.* Edited by Migne. Belgium: Brepols, 1844-55, p. 1196.

Contains the letter to Augustine of Canterbury which outlines Gregory's position on sexuality. See item 185 for a translation of the letter reproduced by Bede. Late sixth century.

200. ———. "Moralia" xxvi, 28. *Patrologiae Cursus Completus, Series Latina 25.* Edited by Migne. Belgium: Brepols, 1844-55, p. 364.

Includes Gregory's views on marital sexuality. Late sixth century.

201. Hildegard of Bingen. "Scivias" *Patrologiae Cursus Completus, Series Latina 197*. Edited by Migne. Belgium: Brepols, 1844-55, pp. 397-98.

Explains prohibition of intercourse during menstruation, arguing that the uterus would reject the sperm during that time. For an excellent analysis of Hildegard's complete theology, see Barbara Newman, item 455. Twelfth century.

202. Honorius. "Epistola 14." *Patrologiae Cursus Completus, Series Latina 80*. Edited by Migne. Belgium: Brepols, 1844-55, p. 841.

Describes prostitutes forcing demands on the governor of Syracuse and notes the appointment of a Bishop as inspector of brothels. Seventh century.

203. Horstmann, Carl, ed. *Nova Legenda Anglie.* vol 1. Oxford: Clarendon Press, 1901.

Contains the Life of Saint Clitaucus which tells of a man and wife whose genitals remained inseparable after intercourse. Fourteenth century.

204. Hroswitha of Gandersheim. "Passion of St. Pelagius." *The Non-dramatic Works of Hroswitha*. Translated by Gonsalva Wiegand. St. Louis: University of St. Louis, 1936.

Describes vividly an attempted homosexual seduction of the young Pelagius by a Muslim king in the "Passion of St. Pelagius." Tenth century.

205. Hugh of St. Victor. "De sacramentis." *Patrologiae Cursus Completus, Series Latina 176*. Edited by Migne. Belgium: Brepols, 1844-55, p. 497.

Builds upon early patristic views of sexuality in comparing appetite for sexual intercourse with that for food. Early twelfth century.

206. Innocent III. "Regestorum Sive Epistolarum." *Patrologiae Cursus Completus, Series Latina*

215. Edited by Migne. Belgium: Brepols, 1844-55, p. 189.

Studies an investigation into the prevalence of sodomy among the clergy. Early thirteenth century.

207. Isidore of Seville. "Differentiarum, Lib. I." *Patrologiae Cursus Completus, Series Latina 83*. Edited by Migne. Belgium: Brepols, 1844-55, p. 37.

Defines and discusses fornication and prostitution in chapter 263. Early seventh century.

208. ———. "De Ecclesiasticis Officiis." *Patrologiae Cursus Completus, Series Latina 83*. Edited by Migne. Belgium: Brepols, 1844-55, pp. 809-14.

Expresses views on marital relations in book II, chapter XX. Early seventh century.

209. ———. *Isidori Hispalensis Episcopi Etymologiarum sive Originum Libri XX*. Edited by W.M. Lindsay. Oxford: Oxford University Press, 1911.

Contains Isidore's explanation of the etymology of genital terms, and is revealing of this influential author's attitudes toward sexuality. See William Sharpe, item 266, for a translation. Early seventh century.

210. Jacob of Verona. *Liber Peregrinationis*. Edited by Ugo Monneret de Villard, Rome: La Libreria della Stato, 1950.

Expresses prevailing notions about sexual excesses of Muslims. Fourteenth century.

211. Jerome. "Epistola 64, ad Fabiolem" *Saint Jerome Lettres,* tom. III. Edited by J. Labourt. Paris: Les Belles Lettres, 1953.

Defines a prostitute in chapter 7. This definition was much quoted throughout the middle ages. Late fourth century.

212. ——. "Vita Pauli." *Patrologiae Cursus Completus, Series Latina 23*. Edited by Migne. Belgium: Brepols, 1844-55, pp.17-30.

Tells of a young man being fondled by a beautiful woman who bit off his tongue to control his desire. Late fourth century.

213. Johannes Vitoduranus."Chronica." *Monumenta Germaniae Historica SS,* New Series III. Edited by F. Baethgen. Berlin: Akademie-Verlag, 1953, pp. 148-50.

Describes the confession of heretical beghards who confess to sexual sins. Fourteenth century.

214. John of Salisbury. *Frivolities of Courtiers and Footprints of Philosophers*. Edited by J.B. Pike. Minneapolis: University of Minnesota Press, 1938.

Warns against prostitution, homosexuality and general lewd conduct in Book III, chapter 13. Twelfth century.

215. ——. *Historia Pontificalis: Memoirs of the Papal Court*. Edited by M. Chibnall. London: Thomas Nelson & Sons, 1956.

Describes a man who died prematurely due to intercourse with his wife against doctor's orders. Twelfth century.

216. Maimonides, Moses. *Guide for the Perplexed.* Translated by Shlomo Pines. Chicago: University of Chicago Press, 1963.

Discusses natural and unnatural intercourse, mentioning bestiality, homosexuality, incest, and prohibitions against intercourse while menstruating. He also recommended circumcision because he believed it would reduce sexual desire for both parties. See particularly Book 3 of the work. Twelfth century.

217. ——. *Maimonides "On Sexual Intercourse fi 'l-jima."* Edited by M. Gorlin. Medical Historical Studies of Medieval Jewish Medical Works, I. New York: Rambash Publications, 1961.

Describes sexual intercourse and the art of loving with more sensitivity to psychological responses than is usually present in medieval medical tracts. Written in the twelfth century and circulated in Latin in the thirteenth century.

218. ——. *Sex Ethics in the Writings of Moses Maimonides.* Translated by Fred Rosner. New York: Bloch Publishing Co., 1974.

Provides an English translation of "Treatise on Cohabitation," and excerpts from other writings by Maimonides on sex. All reveal his belief in the weakening quality of coitus, and its danger to health. Maimonides' work was influential throughout the Middle Ages. Twelfth century.

219. Middleton, Richard. *Commentarium super quarto Sententiarum.* Venice: Bonetus Locatellus, 1499.

Argues that marital sex was no sin, written by a Franciscan theologian. Thirteenth century.

220. *Midrash Rabbah,* 10 vols. Translated by H. Freedman and M. Simon. London: Sonceno Press, 1939.

Presents a Jewish commentary on the Old Testament. Developed from third century B.C. and remained popular and influential throughout the Middle Ages. Early Christian fathers drew from it as did Moslems, and scholastics. Includes discussion of adultery, "unnatural intercourse," bestiality. See especially volumes on Genesis and the Song of Songs.

221. Olivi, Petrus Johannis. "An Virginitas Sit Simpliciter Melior Matrimonio." *Studi Francescani* 64 (1967), 11-57.

Modifies Augustine's view of sex a bit to argue that "innocent" sexuality would be pleasurable. A Franciscan tract. Thirteenth century.

222. ——. "Responsio P.Ioannis ad Aliqua Dicta per Quosdam Magistros Parisiensis de Suis Quaestionibus...." *Archivum Franciscanum Historicum* 28 (1935), 130-55.

Responds to questions posed on marriage and its sacramentality. Franciscan tract that includes his views on sex. Thirteenth century.

223. Peter Cantor. "Verbum Abbreviatum." *Patrologiae Cursus Completus, Series Latina 205*. Edited by Migne. Belgium: Brepols, 1844-55, pp. 333-35.

Preaches against homosexuality and sodomy. A translation may be found in the appendix of Boswell, item 310. Twelfth century.

224. ——. "De vitio sodomitico." *Patrologiae Cursus Completus, Series Latina 205*. Edited by Migne. Belgium: Brepols, 1844-55, pp. 333-35.

Argues that sodomy may be equated with homicide. Twelfth Century.

225. Peter Damian. *Book of Gomorrah: An Eleventh Century Treatise against Clerical Homosexual Practices*. Translated by Pierre J. Payer. Waterloo, Ont: Wilfred Laurier University Press, 1982.

Provides a fine, accessible translation of Peter Damian's influential treatise against clerics indulging in masturbation or homosexual activities. The tract lists the condemned practices and provides insight into some Churchmen's attitudes on sexuality. (See item 226 for an edition of the text). Also contains a clear introduction that establishes the context of the work, and provides a translation of Pope Leo IX's letter responding to Peter's work. Eleventh century.

226. ——. "Liber Gomorrhianus." *Patrologiae Cursus Completus, Series Latina 145*. Edited by Migne. Belgium: Brepols, 1844-55, p. 161.

For a translation, see item 225. Eleventh century.

227. ——. "Opera Omnia-Liber Primus, Epistola XV." *Patrologiae Cursus Completus, Series Latina 144*. Edited by Migne. Belgium: Brepols, 1844-55, pp. 225-35.

Complains of sexually decadent clergy. Eleventh century.

228. ———. "Opuscula Varia." *Patrologiae Cursus Completus, Series Latina 145*. Edited by Migne. Belgium: Brepols, 1844-55, pp. 19-853.

Describes sinful clergy and their activities in numbers 17, 18 and 47. Eleventh century.

229. Peter Lombard. "Libri IV Sententiarum." *Patrologiae Cursus Completus, Series Latina 192*. Edited by Migne. Belgium: Brepols, 1844-55, pp. 519-970.

Describes various forms of lust, including incest and rape. Early twelfth century.

230. Serlo of Bayeux. "Defensio." *Monumenta Germaniae Historica: Libelli de Lite Imperatorum et Pontificum. III* Edited by H. Bohmer and E. Dummler. Hanover: Hahn, 1906-08, pp. 580-83.

Opposes prejudice against priests' sons and accuses those in favor of non-married clergy of sodomy. Early twelfth century.

231. Sextus. *The Sentences of Sextus.* Translated by Richard Edwards, *et al.* Chico, CA: Scholars Press, 1981.

Translates a collection of sayings probably compiled in Egypt in the 2nd century AD, and translated into Latin by Rufinus in the 4th century. That version became popular throughout the early Middle Ages. These sayings offer ethical principles, and some mention lust and sex. Second century.

232. ———. *The Sentences of Sextus: A Contribution to the History of Early Christian Ethics.* Edited by Henry Chadwick. Cambridge: Cambridge University Press, 1959.

Edits the Sentences of Sextus. See the translation by Edwards, item 231. Second century.

233. Sigebert of Gembloux. "Apologia." *Monumenta Germaniae Historica: Libelli de lite Imperatorum et Pontificum* II. Edited by H.

Bohmer and E. Dummler. Hanover: Hahn, 1906-08. pp. 436-48.

Argues for clerical marriage. Includes descriptions of castrations and other violence that accompanied the dispute. Eleventh century.

234. Tertullian. "On Monogamy." *The Ante Nicene Fathers, Vol. 4.* Edited by A. Roberts & J. Donaldson. Grand Rapids: W. B. Eerdmans Publishing Co., 1951, pp. 52-72.

Discusses married sexuality and the nature of the bond that is formed. Also considers adultery. Second century.

235. Thomas of Chobham. *Thomae de Chobham Summa Confessorum.* Edited by F. Broomfield. Paris: Béatrice Nauwelaerts, 1968.

Argues that prostitutes do not sin in getting paid, for they are being paid for labor, not sin. Therefore the church may accept charity from a prostitute. Thirteenth century.

236. Uffing of Werden. "Life of Saint Ida of Herfeld." *Acta Sanctorum Sept II,* Antwerp: Bollandist Society, 1624, pp. 260-69.

Describes Ida having intercourse with her husband, but staying pure by thinking of God at the same time. Eleventh century.

237. "Vita S. Guignerus." *Acta Sanctorum Mar. III.* Antwerp: Bollandist Society, 1645, pp. 459.

Describes an incident in which a couple engaging in sinful intercourse were unable to separate their genitals. Eleventh century.

238. Walafrid of Strabo. "Glossa Ordinaria." *Patrologiae Cursus Completus, Series Latina 113, 114.* Edited by Migne. Belgium: Brepols, 1844-55, pp. 260-62.

Associates sodomy with magic in his gloss on Exodus 22:19. Ninth century.

239. Ward, Benedicta, trans. *Harlots of the Desert.* Kalamazoo: Cistercian Publications, Inc., 1987.

Studies the theme of Christian repentance by translating the Lives of converted prostitutes, Mary Magdalene, Mary of Egypt, Pelagia, Thaïs, and Maria the niece of Abraham. Provides information on prostitution and on transvestism.

240. William Peraldus. *Summa de Vitiis et Virtutibus.* 2 vols. Lyon: Compagnon & Tallandier, 1668.

Thirteenth century.

241. Wyclif, John. "Of the Leaven of Pharisees." *English Works of Wycliff.* Edited by F.D. Matten. London: Kegan Paul, Trench, Trübner & Co., Ltd., 1880.

Accuses friars of sexual sins - adultery, fornication, sodomy and even claims monks use the pretence of medicine to deflower virgins or commit adultery. Fourteenth century.

PRIMARY SOURCES

SCIENCE

This section includes works on medicine and philosophy. Both fields were concerned with understanding the human condition, and both acknowledged that sexuality and sexual acts played an important role in defining that condition. The medical works that discuss reproduction and gynecology made an impact on people's sexual perceptions and actions. For example, the controversy over whether women contributed "seed" during conception or not influenced how people approached intercourse. Those holding the former opinion stressed the importance of female orgasm, those holding the latter did not. The scientific writings were also important because they discussed sexuality with a candor that was often absent in the religious sources. (See Joan Cadden, item 580, for a discussion of scientific sexual openness in an age of purported sexual repression.) I have included works of Aristotle here because his works were so important to the Middle Ages that intellectually they almost belong more to that era than to the ancient world.

242. Albertus Magnus. *Albert the Great, Man and the Beasts: De Animalibus (Books 22-26)*. Translated by James J. Scanlan. Binghamton, NY: Medieval and Renaissance Texts and Studies, 1987.

Translates the last five books of Albertus' *De Animalibus*, in which he departs from Aristotle and adds his own analysis. Book 22 begins with "man," and contains Albert's views on sexuality and reproduction. Includes such topics as the role of imagination in intercourse, priapism, the harmful effects of coitus, aphrodisiacs and contraception. Throughout the tract, Albert describes the reproduction of animals. See item 243 for a complete edition of the text. Thirteenth century.

243. ——. *Alberti Magni Ratisbonensis episcopi, ordinis praedicatorum opera omnia.* 38 vols. Edited by A. Borgnet. Paris: Louis Vives, 1890-99.

Contains Albert's views on human conception in "*De Animalibus,*" books 1, 9, 10, 15, 16, 18, 20, and 22. Within these books he also discusses sexuality and intercourse. (See item 242 for a translation of a portion of this work). Further information may be found in "*Quaestiones de Animalibus,*" for example, see 15,4 for the famous story of a monk who lost his brain tissue through excessive intercourse. See also "*In Evangelium Lucae*" in which he interprets biblical passages that he believed prohibited homosexuality. Thirteenth century.

244. Albertus Magnus (pseudo). *The Book of Secrets of Albertus Magnus.* Edited by Michael R. Best and Frank H. Brightman. Oxford: Clarendon Press, 1973.

Translates a book that had been attributed to Albertus Magnus that tells about uses for certain herbs and stones; for example, some stones cool lust, others act as aphrodisiacs, and still others betray adulterous wives. Thirteenth century.

245. ——. *Secreta Mulierum et Virorum*....Paris: Pierre Gaudol, 1520.

See Lemay, item 686, Kusche, item 678, Ferckel, item 616, and Thorndike, item 795 for discussions of this pseudo-Albertan tract that discusses sexuality.

246. Anthonius Guainerius. *Opera Omnia.* Pavia: n.p., 1481.

Includes the "Tractatus de Matricibus," which describes the proper way to have intercourse so that women may be satisfied, and prescribes masturbation for certain ailments. For an excellent summary of this source, see Helen Rodnite Lemay (item 685). Early fifteenth-century.

247. Aristotle. "Metaphysics." *The Basic Works of Aristotle.* Translated by Richard McKeon. New York: Random House, 1941.

Devotes an entire chapter to considering the ways in which men and women are different, and it is significant that he considered this question central to his analysis of metaphysics.

248. ———. *Generation of Animals*. Translated by A.L. Peck. Cambridge, MA: Harvard University Press, 1943.

Presents Aristotle's view of sexuality and reproduction that assigns women a purely passive, subordinate role. He also describes women, particularly with regard to their sexual organs, as deformed men.

249. Aristotle (pseudo). *Problems*. Translated by W.S. Hett. Cambridge, MA: Loeb Classical Library, 1961.

Expresses, among other things, the widely believed connection between genital organs and eyes and explains the effect of excess intercourse on vision.

250. Arnoldus de Villanova. *Opera*. Lugduni: S. de Gabiano, 1532.

Describes and analyzes various aspects of intercourse, including prescriptions for augmenting desire in women. Late thirteenth or early fourteenth century.

251. Averroës. *Compendia Librorum Aristotelis qui Parva Naturalia Vocantur.* Edited by E.L. Shields and H. Blumberg. Cambridge, MA: Harvard University Press, 1949.

Discusses the effect of sexual intercourse on longevity. Twelfth century.

252. Avicenna. *Canon*. Translated by Gerard of Cremona. Milan: P. de Lavagnia, 1473.

Introduces the Arabic commentator on Aristotle and his medical views, including his description of genitalia. See N.G. Siraisi (item 505) for an accessible discussion of the text. Translated into Latin in the late twelfth century.

253. Burton, L.L. "Sidrak on Reproduction and Sexual Love." *Medical History* 19 (1975): 286-302.

Corrects the text of the edition of the Middle English dialogue *Sidrak and Bokkus* edited by Nichols (item 273). Compares the manuscript used by Nichols with other redactions, including early French ones. Discusses such matters as the semen potency of a lecherous man, the best sort of woman for sexual pleasure, and the relative sexual capacity of men and women. Fourteenth century.

254. Caelius Aurelianus. *Gynaecia.* Edited by M.F. Drabkin. Baltimore: Johns Hopkins Press, 1951.

Presents a Latin version of Soranus' *Gynecology* from a thirteenth-century manuscript fragment. Original text from the second century.

255. Colonnia, Egidio. *De Formatione Humani Corporis Egidii Romani.* Venetiis; Impresum per Jacobum Pentium de Leuco, 1523.

Medical text describing gynecological theory. Late twelfth century.

256. Constantinus Africanus. *Constantini Liber de Coitu: El Tratado de Andrologia de Constantino el Africano.* Edited by E. Montero Cartelle. Santiago de Compostella: Universidad de Santiago de Compostella, 1983.

Presents an edition of the medical tract "On Intercourse." This tract contains detailed discussion and recommendations on coitus, and is indispensable for a study on medieval sexuality. Good edition with introductory material. See item 257 for an English translation, and item 259 for an Italian translation with detailed analysis. Eleventh century.

257. ———. "De Coitu." Translated by Paul Delany. *Chaucer Review* 4 (1970), 55-65.

Translates a text on fertility and intercourse. It includes a discussion of kinds of semen, varieties in male sexual characteristics, conditions conducive for intercourse, effects of intercourse and aphrodisiacs. See item 256 for an edition. Eleventh century.

258. ——. "The De Genecia Attributed to Constantine the African." Edited by Monica H. Green. *Speculum* 62 (Apr.1987): 299-323.

Deals with the structure of the womb and other female reproductive organs, their function in conception and birth, the anatomy of the breasts, and final chapters on testes, ovaries, and penises. Eleventh century.

259. ——. *Il Trattato di fisiologia e igiena sessuale.* Translated by Marco T. Malato. Rome: Istituto di Storia della Medicina, 1962.

Includes a translation and commentary on "De Coitu." Eleventh century.

260. Corner, George W., trans. *Anatomical Texts of the Earlier Middle Ages.* Washington: National Publishing Company, 1927.

Presents a collection of medical anatomy texts from Salerno. Early twelfth century.

261. Galen (pseudo). *"Microtegni seu De Spermate," Traduzione e Commento.* Translated by V. Passalacqua. Rome: Istituto di Storia della medicina dell'Università di Roma, 1958.

Offers an Italian translation of a widely circulated medical text that adhered to the seven-cell theory of the uterus. Twelfth century.

262. Gilbertus Anglicus. *Gilbertus Anglicus, Medicine of the Thirteenth Century.* Edited by Henry E. Handerson. Cleveland: Medical Library Association, 1918.

Attributes diseases such as arthritis and gout to sexual excess. Thirteenth century.

263. Hargreaves, Henry. "De Spermate Hominis." *Medieval Studies* 39 (1977): 506-10.

Edits a Middle English poem on conception and embryology. While not memorable poetry, it presents a valuable contribution to an understanding of medieval medical opinion. Mid-fifteenth century.

264. Hildegard of Bingen. *Causae et Curae.* Edited by Paul Kaiser. Leipzig: Teubner, 1903.

Presents an edition of Hildegard of Bingen's medical tract with its discussion of sex and sexual characteristics of men and women. For an excellent summary and analysis of this work, see Joan Cadden (item 579). Further information about Hildegard may be found in Barbara Newman (item 455). Twelfth century.

265. Hoffman, G. "Beiträge zur Lehre von der durch Zauber verursachten Krankheit und ihrer Behandlung in der Medizin des Mittelalters." *Janus* 37 (1933): pp. 191-92.

Includes the text of Guy of Chauliac's description of how a doctor may ascertain whether a man is impotent. Fourteenth century.

266. Isidore of Seville. *Isidore of Seville: The Medical Writings. An English Translation with an Introduction and Commentary.* Translated by William D. Sharpe. Philadelphia: Transactions of the American Philosophical Society, n.s., LIV-2, 1964.

Translates excerpts from Isidore's *Etymologies.* Compare with the edition of Lindsay, item 209. Early seventh century.

267. John of Gaddesdon. *Rosa Anglica.* Edited by Winifred Wulff. London: Simpkin Marshall, Ltd., 1929.

Offers advice on how to avoid catching venereal disease after coitus. Early fourteenth century.

268. Lawn, Brian, ed. *The Prose Salernitan Questions.* London: Oxford University Press, 1979.

Presents an edition of an English manuscript that poses and answers questions on medicine and natural science. The editor notes the compiler was "unusually preoccupied with sexual matters and gynecology." Well indexed to make an excellent, accessible source. Late twelfth or early thirteenth century.

269. Mondino da Luzzi. *"Anathomia" The Fasciculus Medicinae of Joannes de Ketham.* Edited by Charles Singer. Milan: R. Lier and Co., 1924.

Discusses sexuality and the anatomy of sexual organs based on early dissections. Early fourteenth century.

270. Montero Cartelle, E., ed. *Liber Minor de Coitu: Tratado Menor de Andrologia Anonimo Salernitano.* Valladolid: Universidad de Valladolid, 1987.

Presents an edition of an interesting and little-known anonymous medical treatise on intercourse. This treatise is unusual because it is specifically about coitus, without focusing on reproduction as the desired result. Discusses excessive intercourse, positions, aphrodisiacs, and diseases. About twelfth century.

271. Moschion. *La "Gynaecia" di Moschione: Manuale per le Ostetriche e le Mamme del VI Sec. d. C.* Edited by R. Radicchi. Pisa: Editrice Giardini, 1970.

Describes the genitals, including the clitoris (unusual in early medieval medical tracts). Sixth century.

272. Muntner, Suessmann, ed. *Sexual Life (Hygiene and its Medical Treatment): Collection of Mediaeval Treatises.* Jerusalem: Geniza Publishing Co., 1965.

Collects Hebrew texts that contain medical information on sex in the Middle Ages. Includes Maimonides' "Secrets of Sexual Life," and Ubeid Ibn Ali G'urgana's "On Sexual Weakness." In Hebrew with a short English preface.

273. Nichols, Robert E., Jr. "Procreation, Pregnancy, and Parturition: Extracts from a Middle English Metrical Encyclopedia." *Medical History* 11 (1967): 175-81.

Translates portions of a manuscript that discusses intercourse and pregnancy. For a corrected text, see Burton, item 253. Fifteenth century.

274. Petrus Hispanus. *Obras Médicas de Pedro Hispano.* Edited by M. Helena da Rocha Pereira. Coimbra: Por Ordem da Universidade, 1973.

Presents a fine edition of Pope John XXI's medical writings and includes a Portuguese translation. The source deals with topics such as problems with the penis, aphrodisiacs and anaphrodisiacs. Thirteenth century.

275. Rowland, Beryl, trans. *Medieval Woman's Guide to Health: The First English Gynecological Handbook.* Kent, OH; Kent State University Press, 1981.

Contributes an edition and translation of a Middle English manuscript (Sloane 2463) that was based on the Latin treatise by Trotula. It contains, among other things, a prescription of intercourse as a cure for a particular uterine malady, and a series of anaphrodisiacs to prevent erections. This edition is not only excellent in itself, but contains a complete bibliography of primary and secondary sources on medieval medicine in general and gynecology in particular. Early fifteenth century.

276. Singer, Charles, trans. "A Thirteenth-Century Description of Leprosy." *Journal of the History of Medicine,* 4 (1949): 237-39.

Offers an edition and translation of a portion of manuscript 1398 in the Bodleian Library at Oxford which contains an unusually detailed description of leprosy. Includes the typical medieval association between leprosy and sexuality by noting that a person may get the disease by "lying with a woman with whom a leper has lain," and by claiming that lepers are anxious to have sexual intercourse with the healthy. Thirteenth century.

277. ——. "A Thirteenth-Century Drawing of the Anatomy of the Uterus and Adnexa." *Proceedings of the Royal Society of Medicine* 9 (1916), 44-5.

278. Soranus. *Gynecology.* Edited by Temkin Owsei. Baltimore: Johns Hopkins Press, 1956.

Discusses in detail female anatomy, conception, childbirth and the diseases that afflict female genital organs. Soranus was a famous physician of the early second century in the Roman Empire. I include this translation of his famous work on gynecology (which includes detailed information on obstetrics as well) because it was a predominate force in the medieval West until the eleventh century when Galen's work took precedence.

279. Steinber, Werner & Suessmann Muntner. "Maimonides' Views on Gynecology and Obstetrics: English Translation of Chapter Sixteen of his Treatise, 'Pirke Moshe' (Medical Aphorisms)." *American Journal of Obstetrics and Gynecology* 91 (1965): 443-48.

Translates Maimonides' aphorisms that were originally written in Arabic and translated in the thirteenth century into medieval Hebrew. Includes opinions on what causes desire for intercourse and the medical benefit of orgasms given women by midwives. Twelfth century.

280. Thomas Aquinas. *Commentary on the 'Metaphysics' of Aristotle*. Translated by John P. Rowan. Chicago: Henry Regnery, 1961.

Thirteenth century.

281. ——. *On the Power of God*. Translated by the English Dominican Fathers. Westminster, MD: Newman Press, 1952.

Includes his views on reproduction which follow Aristotle. Also reflects upon demons' capacities to transport human semen to impregnate women, and considers the paternity of children thus conceived. Thirteenth century.

282. ——. *Truth.* 3 vols. Translated by Robert W. Mulligan. Chicago: Henry Regnery Co., 1952.

Includes his views on reproduction and intercourse. See especially vol. 3 on sensuality and the passions. Thirteenth century.

283. ——. *Summa Theologiae*. Translated by the English Dominican Fathers. New York: Benzigen Bros., Inc., 1947.

Contains information on sexuality throughout the tract, but for some typical entries, see the following questions: Question 154 on the parts of lust, which includes a discussion on fornication, adultery, incest, seduction, rape, nocturnal emissions, masturbation (which he calls the sin of "effeminacy"), bestiality and sodomy; Part II, question 46 for consent versus consummation in marriage; question 58 for impotence and spells that can cause it; question 81 on sensuality. Thirteenth century.

284. Trotula of Salerno. *The Diseases of Women.* Edited by E. Mason-Hohl. Los Angeles: Ward Ritchie Press, 1940.

Translates a medical tract attributed to a woman physician, Trotula, which among other things, recognized that infertility was as often the man's fault as the women's. Provides remedies for infertility in both men and women, offering recommendations for timing and technique of intercourse. It also includes birth control methods. This translation is accessible, but since it is a fairly free translation, it should not be used by those needing precision in language from the original. Eleventh century.

285. Vernet, J. "Los Médicos Andaluces en el *Libro de las Generaciones de Médicos,* - ibn Yulyul." *Anuario de Estudios Medievales* 5 (1968): pp. 456-7.

Includes an anecdote describing the results of bestiality. Tenth century.

286. Vincent of Beauvais. *Speculum Maius*. 4 vols. Graz: Akademische Druck- u Verlag, 1964-5.

Devotes a whole chapter (xxxi,26) to why prostitutes rarely conceive. See also vol. 2 pp. 916-17, and vol 3, p. 1372, for his arguments against sodomy. Also contains medical information. Thirteenth century.

287. Wack, Mary Frances. "The Liber de heros morbo of Johannes Afflacius and its Implications for Medieval Love Conventions." *Speculum* 62 (Apr.1987): 324-44.

Provides an edition and translation of the *Liber de Heros Morbo* that was translated from Arabic in about 1100. This text describes lovesickness as a medical problem, and prescribes various treatments, including intercourse with someone other than the obsessive object. Dr. Wack offers the intriguing suggestion that this text influenced the conventions of courtly love by providing a medical justification for the ideals of emotion that were supposed to govern a chivalrous lover. Twelfth century.

288. Wickersheimer, E. *Manuscrits Latins de Médecine du haut Moyen Age dans les Bibliothèques de France*. Paris: CNRS, 1966.

Describes medieval medical contraceptive recipes.

289. William of Conches. *Dialogus de Substantiis*. Starsbourg: J. Rihelius, 1567.

Discusses anatomy and physiology of sexuality, and includes an analysis of the effects of prostitution and rape on women's sexual responses. Twelfth century.

SECONDARY SOURCES

SECONDARY SOURCES

BOOKS

290. Adams, James N. *The Latin Sexual Vocabulary*. Baltimore: Johns Hopkins Press, 1982.

Discusses sexual terms used in Latin. This well-researched and scholarly work includes words and metaphors for genitals as well as intercourse (including oral and anal). While the work deals primarily with the classical sources, it does contain some discussion of medieval works. It is useful as a preliminary for a study of medieval sexuality to clarify the frequently ambiguous Latin words.

291. Alesandro, John A. *Gratian's Notion of Marital Consummation*. Rome: Officium Libri Catholici, 1971.

Provides an excellent summary of Gratian's views on marital consummation, including his ideas on fornication and incest. (The modern reader should keep in mind that incest in this context included anything within a wide degree of consanguinity.)

292. Aliotta, Maurizio. *La Teologia del Peccato in Alano di Lilla*. Palermo: Augustinus, 1986.

Analyzes a source that is often used in the study of medieval sexuality, and while the organization of the book as a whole is somewhat awkward, and the analysis somewhat unclear, the fourth and fifth chapters deal directly with Alan of Lille's description and categorization of sin and contain some useful information.

293. Allen, Prudence. *The Concept of Woman: The Aristotelian Revolution, 750 BC-AD 1250.* Montreal: Eden Press, 1985.

Studies clearly and comprehensively the history of philosophic discussions of the nature of women and the relationship between men and women. The author considers classical and medieval schools of philosophy in terms of whether they advocated a position of "sex unity, sex polarity or sex complementarity" on gender issues. Within this enlightening discussion of gender, the author illuminates the treatment of sexuality, intercourse and reproduction by Aristotle, Hildegard of Bingen and others.

294. Andersen, Jørgen. *The Witch on the Wall: Erotic Sculpture in the British Isles.* Copenhagen: Rosenkilde & Bagger, 1977.

Describes sculptures in England and Ireland dating from the twelfth through the early sixteenth centuries that portray stylized women with their legs spread apart calling attention to their genitals. Cautiously discusses some explanations for these figures, suggesting they might be fertility figures or protective totems.

295. Ariés, Philippe and A. Bejin, eds. *Western Sexuality: Practice and Precept in Past and Present Times*. Oxford: Basil Blackwell, 1985.

Collects a thought-provoking series of essays on various topics of sexuality, including several medieval ones, such as St. Paul's view of the Flesh, prostitution in 15th century France, and sex and love in married life. A worthwhile survey.

296. Baer, Richard A. Jr. *Philo's Use of the Categories Male and Female*. Leiden, Netherlands: E.J. Brill, 1970.

Discusses aspects of Philo's thought that influenced subsequent patristic notions on sexuality. Particularly relevant is II, C , "Man's Lower Nature: the Realm of Male and Female." This is a scholarly and thoughtful work.

297. Bailey, Derrick Sherwin. *Homosexuality and the Western Christian Tradition*. New York: Longmans, Green & Co., 1955.

Studies the Western Christian tradition concerning homosexuality from Biblical references through the early Middle Ages. It is a detailed, well-researched survey that was written with the explicit goal to ameliorate the British laws against homosexuality by demonstrating that most of them have no basis in Scripture.

298. ———. *Sexual Relations in Christian Thought*. New York: Harper & Brothers, 1959.

Offers a general survey of the subject, but the work is too dated and broad.

299. Barber, Malcolm. *The Trial of the Templars*. Cambridge: Cambridge University Press, 1978.

Argues that the charges against the Templars of homosexuality and sexual orgies had no basis in fact, but were designed to play on the fears of their contemporaries.

300. Barthélemy, Loris. *La Prostitution à Marseille pendant le moyen-âge*. Marseille: Cayer & Cíe, 1883.

Continues the collection of documents on prostitution and venereal disease in Marseille begun by Mireur, item 23.

301. Basserman, Lujo. *The Oldest Profession: A History of Prostitution*. Translated by J. Cleugh. New York: Stein and Day, 1968.

Purports to offer a summary of the history of prostitution from the classical world through World War II. The section on the Middle Ages is superficial and provides no solid information. The author merely draws on anecdotes from Villon, Louis IX and others who refer to prostitution, but provides no analysis, citations or bibliography. A popular account, useless for the scholar.

302. Bellamy, John. *Crime and Public Order in England in the Later Middle Ages*. Toronto: University of Toronto Press, 1973.

Studies crime and its prosecution and punishment in late medieval England, and includes information on rape, prostitution and fornication. The evidence is drawn mostly from trial records and legal documents. This is a thorough and important work.

303. Bernheimer, R. *Wild Men in the Middle Ages: A Study in Art, Sentiment, and Demonology*. Cambridge, Mass: Harvard University Press, 1952.

Argues that the prevalent "wild man" motif in the late Middle Ages was a projection of men's desires, so in erotic contexts, he expresses raw lust. See especially the chapter on "Erotic Connotations."

304. Bleibtreu-Ehrenberg, Gisela. *Tabu Homosexualität: die Geschichte eines Vorurteils*. Frankfurt am Maïn: S. Fischer, 1978.

Studies the development of attitudes toward male homosexuality from the early Germanic tribal period to the Inquisition in the late Middle Ages. In this impressively thorough study, the author draws from church and secular laws, Germanic sagas and other sources to show the effect of increasingly repressive attitudes toward homosexuality, transvestism and other sexual variations.

305. Bloch, Iwan. *Die Prostitution.* 2 vols. Berlin: L. Marcus, 1912 & 1925.

Contains a classic, but dated, discussion on prostitution. Volume 1 discusses the Middle Ages.

306. ——. *Sexual Life in England, Past and Present.* London: Aldor, 1938.

307. Bloch, R. Howard. *The Scandal of the Fabliaux.* Chicago: University of Chicago Press, 1986.

Reevaluates fabliaux studies, and looks at the use of language in the stories to demonstrate that the tales are more sophisticated narratives than had previously been credited. He also attacks the idea that the fabliaux can be used as historical sources for sexual practices. He prefers to see them in the light of Freudian (and post-Freudian) analysis. This argument might be read in conjunction with that of Muscatine, item 454, who takes a more historical approach.

308. Bolen, Carl von. *Geschichte der Erotik*. Wien: Verlag Willy Verkauf, 1951.

Offers a history of eroticism from antiquity to modern times, and for the Middle Ages, focuses on the influence of church teaching on sexuality and on perceptions of witchcraft. This book is written from a feminist point of view, arguing that women have not been allowed to be sexually expressive. It includes a discussion of lesbianism, which is rare in the literature. Unfortunately, the solid scholarship is weakened by a presentation that is overly polemical.

309. Bonilla García, Luis. *El Amor y su Alcance Histórico Revista de Occidente*. Madrid: Revista de Occidente, 1964.

Summarizes generally the history of love from the ancient Greeks through the 19th century and contains three chapters on the Middle Ages. The work focuses mainly on Spain, although it occasionally draws from other regions. The author primarily uses literary sources, although he does at times consider legal documents. The book is too general and unfocused to be of much use to any but those with the most casual interest.

310. Boswell, John. *Christianity, Social Tolerance and Homosexuality*. Chicago: University of Chicago Press, 1980.

Argues that intolerance of homosexuality did not derive from Christianity but from the social and intellectual context of the thirteenth century. This is a pathbreaking work that has generated much controversy. It shows an impressive use of the sources and is valuable for the range of information it provides on the subject of homosexuality. The thesis is suggestive, but remains unproven. Boswell demonstrates that the thirteenth century was restrictive, but he is less convincing on the attitudes of the early Middle Ages. Nevertheless, this book is essential reading for anyone interested in the subject.

311. ——. *Rediscovering Gay History: Archetypes of Gay Love in Christian History*. London: Gay Christian Movement, 1982.

Presents in pamphlet form a suggestive hypothesis that condemnation of homosexual love grew out of a general condemnation of any love outside marriage that emerged as a reaction to the twelfth century cult of courtly love. However, the thesis remains to be proven, for this essay lacks the detailed evidence that marks Boswell's larger work (item 310). However, he does include a ceremony marking "spiritual friendship" that Boswell suggests is a prototype of gay marriage.

312. ——. *The Royal Treasure: Muslim Communities under the Crown of Aragon in the Fourteenth Century.* New Haven: Yale University Press, 1977.

Includes information about prostitution in fourteenth-century Spain, and contains editions of documents on prostitution in the appendix. There is little work available on prostitution in the Iberian peninsula, and Boswell is an excellent guide to the unpublished sources.

313. Boulting, William. *Women in Italy from the Introduction of the Chivalrous Service of Love to the...Professional Actress*. London: Metheun & Co., 1910.

Mentions the late medieval practices of adultery, public proof of male virility, prostitution and rape. Argues (without much evidence) that Renaissance sexual licence was but the continuation of medieval morality. This book is too dated to be of much use.

314. Bourke, J.G. *Scatologic Rites of All Nations.* Washington, D.C.: Lowdermilk, 1891.

315. Brandl, Leopold. *Die Sexualethik des Heiligen Albertus Magnus*. Regensburg: Verlag Friedrich Pustet, 1955.

Studies sexual ethics in Albert the Great and discusses the place of lust within this ethic. The author traces the influences of Augustine, Aristotle and Hugh of St. Victor, and analyzes the hierarchy of sinfulness of various sexual practices in Albert's thought.

316. Briffault, Robert. *The Mothers: A Study of the Origins of Sentiments and Institutions* 3 vols. New York: Macmillan Company, 1927.

Presents a social anthropological study of marriage, sex, family, and the role of women. Draws from evidence from primitive tribes as well as historical figures to argue that the "female instincts" are central to social organization, and to urge women to embrace those "instincts." Volume 3 analyzes Medieval Europe, arguing without much evidence that the early Celts and Germans were sexually free, and that the Middle Ages showed a development toward more repression. A dated, highly idiosyncratic essay.

317. ——. *Sin and Sex*. New York: Haskell House, 1973.

Reprints a 1931 book containing one chapter on the Middle Ages, entitled "Christian Sexophobia." It is yet one more biased polemic against excessive patristic morality.

318. Brody, Saul Nathaniel. *The Disease of the Soul, Leprosy in Medieval Literature*. Ithaca, NY: Cornell University Press, 1974.

Describes the medieval associations of leprosy with sin and sex. Includes medical authorities, who considered leprosy a venereal disease, ecclesiastical authorities, who saw leprosy as a metaphor for lust, and literary writers, who also associated lepers with lust. This is a fine, well-argued book.

319. Browe, Peter. *Beiträge zur Sexualethik des Mittelalters*. Breslau: Breslauer Studien zur H. T., 1932.

Discusses briefly the Church Fathers', canon lawyers' and scholastics' views on marriage and intercourse. Contains nothing that cannot be more readily found elsewhere.

320. ——. *Zur Geschichte der Entmannung*. Breslau: Müller & Seiffert, 1936.

321. Brown, Peter R.L. *The Body and Society: Men, Women, and Sexual Renunciation in Early Christianity*. New York: Columbia University Press, 1988.

Traces the changing ideas about sexuality and chastity in late antiquity, from St. Paul to Augustine. In elegant prose, Brown describes the conflicting beliefs about the role of sexuality in a Christian world, ranging from Encratite insistence on chastity to praise of temperate sex in Christian marriages. Perhaps the most significant contribution of this book is Brown's articulation of the change in perception of the role of the individual's body, did it belong to the public sphere of the city, or the private sphere of the individual or family? The Christian revolution marked the victory of the latter. This will remain a significant work in the field.

322. Brownmiller, Susan. *Against Our Will: Men, Women and Rape*. New York: Simon and Schuster, 1975.

Argues that rape is not an occasional aberrant, violent act, but fundamental to the relationship between men and women throughout history. Includes some information about the Middle Ages (anecdotes and rape laws), but the presentation is too general to serve as a historical resource. However, this controversial and influential book has articulated a theoretical view of rape that shapes further studies.

323. Brundage, James. *Law, Sex and Christian Society in Medieval Europe*. Chicago: University of Chicago Press, 1987.

Offers a detailed analysis of the development of sex law from the ancient world to the Reformation, with particular focus on the development of sexual legislation in canon law. The thesis is that the Gregorian reformers of the eleventh century converted church doctrines about sex into legal prescriptions, which then moved into canon law and secular law and have penetrated our own laws. This work contains an important analysis of the relationship between sex, law and theology, and is likely to become a classic.

324. Brussendorff, Ove and Poul Hanningson. *A History of Eroticism,* 6 vols. Copenhagen: Veta Publishers, 1963.

Introduces an anecdotal survey of some aspects of the history of prostitution interwoven with some famous scandals and erotic literary works. Volume two covers the Middle Ages to the eighteenth century. The medieval period includes chapters on early patristic preoccupation with chastity, prostitution in the Middle Ages, and the story of Abelard and Heloïse. Not a scholarly work, and the brief text seems only to form a backdrop for the extensive illustrations.

325. Bullough, Vern L. *Bibliography of Prostitution.* New York: Garland Publishing, 1977.

Includes a section on the history of prostitution, but this should be supplemented with the bibliography in a more current work, for example that of Otis (item 460).

326. ——. *The History of Prostitution.* New York: University Books, 1964.

Describes famous prostitutes and great men who were involved with prostitutes. This collection approaches the study of prostitution from the point of view of individuals, providing a supplement to the more usual approach in works that deal with the structure of prostitution. Contains several chapters on the Middle Ages, and argues that prostitution flourishes where men spend time away from families, where there is a strong "double standard," and where there are impediments to marriages. A solid general work that paved the way for future studies.

327. ——. *Sex, Society and History.* New York: Science History Publications, 1976.

Reprints a number of Bullough's articles that appeared in several journals. Includes three good articles on medieval history of sexuality.

328. Bullough, Vern L. and James Brundage. *Sexual Practices and the Medieval Church.* Buffalo, NY: Prometheus Books, 1982.

Collects eighteen essays on various topics related to sexuality in the Middle Ages. Includes articles on prostitution, transvestism, homosexuality, sex and canon law, and sexuality in scientific writings.

329. ———. *Sexual Variance in Society and History*. New York: John Wiley & Sons, Inc., 1976.

Surveys a wider field than just medieval, although it does include a section on the Greco-Roman and early Christian attitudes toward sexuality, and another section on the Middle Ages. The cross-cultural and wider time span of this book provides good comparative material for medieval studies of sexuality.

330. ———. *The Subordinate Sex.* Urbana, IL: University of Illinois Press, 1973.

Surveys the history of women from the classical world through the industrial world primarily in the West, although it contains chapters on Islam, China and India. Since the history of women is often linked to attitudes toward sexuality, Bullough's book includes such material. He discusses Aristotle's medical views, patristic anti-sexual polemics, Islamic sexual acceptance, and the conventions of courtly love. Offers a solid, general survey of the topics.

331. Burford, E.J. *Bawds and Lodgings.* London: Peter Owen, Ltd., 1976.

Studies the history of London's brothel district on Bankside in Southwark from Roman times through the seventeenth century. A popularized, highly speculative account, and the endnotes are sparse, documenting the obvious while leaving the more dubious claims unproven. It does contain an edition of the important twelfth-century ordinance regulating the brothels of Southwark.

332. ———. *The Orrible Synne, A Look at London Lechery from Roman to Cromwellian Times.* London: P. Owen, 1973.

Proffers an unscholarly account of London vices, but does include a list of primary-source editions of documents providing information on prostitution in Britain.

333. Buschan, George. *Das deutsche Volk in Sitte und Brauch unter Mitwirkung von Max Bauer.* Stuttgart: Union Deutsche Verlagsgesellschaft, 1922.

334. Buschinger Danielle and André Crépin, editors. *Amour, Mariage et Transgressions au Moyen Age.* Göppingen: Kümmerle Verlag, 1984.

Collects forty-three short articles on such subjects as incest (Charlemagne's and others'), rape, homosexuality, adultery, etc. All deal with literary evidence, so the articles speak to literary, not historical, treatment. Nevertheless, the collection is unusual and provides a broad view of sexuality in medieval literature.

335. ———. *Comique, satire et Parodie dans la Tradition Renardienne et les Fabliaux.* Actes du colloque des 15 et 16 janvier 1983. Göppingen: Kümmerle Verlag, 1983.

Presents papers on the subject of humor in the fabliaux and beast epics, including the use of scatological humor.

336. Buttitta, Antonio, editor. *Classici della Cultura Siciliana.* Palermo: S.F. Flaccovio, Editore, 1971.

Reprints a 1903 monograph on prostitution in Sicily originally written by Antonio Cutrera that looks at the subject from historical and legal documents. Includes editions of documents.

337. Büttner, Theodora and Ernst Werner. *Circumcellionen und Adamiten: Zwei Form mittealterich Haeresie.* Berlin: Akademia Verlag, 1959.

Argues that heretical antinomianism is a statement of rebellion against hypocrisy.

338. Campbell, G.A. *The Knights Templars, Their Rise and Fall.* New York: Robert McBride, 1937.

Discusses the charges against the Templars, including sodomy and homosexuality.

339. Cantalamessa, Raniero. *Etica Sessuale e matrimonio nel cristianesimo delle origini.* Milan: Università Cattolica del Sacro Cuore, 1976.

Presents a collection of essays on the general topics of marriage and sexual ethics during the early centuries of Christianity. Includes discussions of sexual ethics in canon law, sexuality, concupiscence and marriage in the works of Augustine. A well-conceived volume that approaches the subject objectively.

340. Capelli, Giovanni. *Autoerotismo: Un problema morale nei primi secoli cristiani?* Bologna: Centro Editoriale Dehoniano, 1986.

Surveys the prohibition of masturbation from the first centuries of Christianity to the end of the first millennium. Includes biblical, stoic, gnostic, patristic and penitential works. Offers the argument that masturbation only became a specific prohibition in the sixth century, with the Irish and English penitentials. A thought-provoking monograph, but more work on the early sources needs to be done for the thesis to be fully accepted.

341. Carter, John Marshall. *Rape in Medieval England.* New York: University Press of America, 1985.

Approaches the study of rape in thirteenth-century England from an historical and sociological view. Bases his analysis primarily on the Eyre Rolls and other legal sources. Argues, among other things, that rape was not widely recorded due to the difficulties of proving the crime and the humiliation of the victim. Unfortunately, the work is marred by some careless interpretation and scholarship. This work might be most usefully used as an introduction to the Eyre Rolls.

342. Cartoux, Georges. *Condition des Courtisans à Avignon du XIIe au XIXe Siècle.* Lyon: A. Rey, 1925.

343. Casas, Enrique. *Las Ceremonias Nupciales.* Madrid: Editorial Paez, 1926.

Surveys various sexual practices from a cross-cultural perspective. Includes some medieval information, but the work is too general to be of more than superficial interest.

344. Charasson, A. *Un Curé Plébéien au XIIe siècle: Foulques, Curé de Neuilly-sur-Marne (1191-1202).* Paris: F.R. de Rudeval, 1905.

Compare with Gutsch, item 635, who discusses the same text.

345. Chydenius, John. *Love and the Medieval Tradition.* Helsinki: Societas Scientiarum Fennica, 1977.

Presents a philosophical analysis of the various types of love found in the medieval tradition. Sexual love, stripped of allegory, he identifies as "passionism" and traces its articulation to Héloïse. The argument does not have enough depth or breadth to be particularly significant historically.

346. Cleugh, James. *Love Locked Out: A Survey of Love, License, and Restrictions in the Middle Ages.* London: Anthony Blond, 1963.

Affords a chatty, easy to read discussion of "love, licence and restriction in the Middle Ages" which, while at times accurate, is virtually useless for any scholarly analysis since it lacks documentation of evidence and persuasiveness of argument. It purports to demonstrate that ecclesiastical repression led to extreme licentiousness during the Middle Ages, a thesis that remains unproven.

347. Cohn, Norman. *Europe's Inner Demons.* New York: Meridian Press, 1975.

Traces the development of the idea of witchcraft to a level sufficient to trigger the witch trials that began in earnest in the fifteenth century. This work cannot serve as the definitive study of witchcraft, but it does shed light on medieval attitudes toward sexuality as people slowly attributed orgies and intercourse with the Devil to witches. Cohn's hypothesis that "tales of...promiscuous orgies...reflect repressed desires, or if one prefers, feared temptations" may not be completely demonstrated here, but it deserves consideration.

348. Conrad, Hermann. *Deutsche Rechtsgeschichte. Frühzeit und Mittelalter.* Karlsruhe: C. F. Müller, 1962.

Surveys comprehensively the history of law in Germany as developed from the Germanic law codes. Within the larger discussion, the author includes analysis of punishment for sexual crimes such as rape, sodomy and "unnatural sexual practices."

349. Cooke, T.D., and B. L. Honeycutt, editors. *The Humor of the Fabliaux: A Collection of Critical Essays*. Columbia: University of Missouri Press, 1974.

Collects essays on the fabliaux. For the study of sexuality see especially, Thomas D. Cooke, "Pornography, the Comic Spirit and the Fabliaux" and Roy J. Pearcy, "Modes of Signification and the Humor of Obscene Diction in the Fabliaux." These articles are also helpful in guiding the reader to the tales that deal most directly with sexuality.

350. Coriden, Jacobo A. *The Indissolubility Added to Christian Marriage by Consummation*. Rome: Officium Libri Catholici, 1961.

Investigates the development of the importance of consummation as critical to the indissolubility of the marriage bond in the eyes of the Catholic Church. This work analyzes church teaching (particularly the canon lawyers) from the eighth century through the pontificate of Innocent III in the early thirteenth century. The work is thorough, but the same material is more easily accessible in Brundage (item 323).

351. Cosby, Michael R. *Sex in the Bible*. Englewood Cliffs, NJ: Prentice-Hall, Inc., 1984.

Summarizes biblical references to sexual practices and attitudes. While it does not deal directly with the Middle Ages, it does give a clear explanation of the materials that the medieval thinkers were drawing upon in their analysis of sexual mores. As such, it provides substantial background. This is a short, useful work written for the non-scholarly audience.

352. Couture, Roger A. *L'Imputabilité Morale des Premiers Mouvements de Sensualité de Saint Thomas aux Salmanticenses*. Roma: Presses de l'Université Grégorienne, 1962.

Considers the development of church doctrine about the sinfulness of "sexual movements" not controlled by reason. Begins with Scholastic reflections on this subject in the twelfth and thirteenth centuries and pursues it through the seventeenth century.

353. Curry, Walter Clyde. *Chaucer and the Mediaeval Sciences*. New York: Barnes & Noble, 1960.

Argues that the Pardoner is a congenital eunuch because he has the physical attributes of a eunuch as described in physiognomy texts available to Chaucer. Further maintains that the Summoner has leprosy associated with his "lechery." Some of the conclusions may be disputed, but the discussion provides much information on medieval views of sexuality from the points of view of medicine, astrology and physiognomy.

354. Cutner, Herbert. *A Short History of Sex Worship*. London: Watts & Co., 1950.

Surveys briefly phallic worship from the ancient Middle East and ancient Judaism, through classical Rome and Christian Europe, with a short digression to India. This is highly speculative and lacks scholarly citations and support, but represents an interesting exercise in demonstrating that virtually all religious symbols and words can be interpreted sexually.

355. Daichman, Graciela S. *Wayward Nuns in Medieval Literature*. Syracuse, NY: Syracuse University Press, 1986.

Studies primarily the literary treatment of wayward nuns in the Middle Ages (with some historical background) that led up to the fourteenth-century descriptions of Chaucer's Madame Eglentyne and the Archpriest of Hita's Doña Garoza in the *Libro de Buen Amor.* The author's material is detailed and carefully presented, but since it was selected to provide background for the two fictional characters, it is limited in scope. Additionally, the historical material is not well selected and is inadequate. For example, there is no discussion of historical Spain, yet one of the sources that is the focus of this subject is from Spain.

356. Darmon, P. *Le Tribunal de l'impuissance, virilité et défaillances conjugales dans l'Ancienne France.* Paris: Seuil, 1979.

Discusses impotence as a grounds for marriage annulment.

357. Dauvillier, J. *Le Mariage dans le Droit Classique de l'Eglise depuis le Décret de Gratien (1140)* .... Paris: Recueil Suey, 1933.

Describes canon law on marriage from Gratian to the death of Clement V (1314). It deals mostly with marriage, but it does have sections on impotence as a marital impediment and consummation of marriage. All this material is more accessibly covered by Brundage, item 323.

358. Delannoy, J.C. *Pécheresses et Repenties: Notes pour Servir à l'Histoire de la Prostitution à Amiens du XIVe au XIXe Siècle.* Amiens: Impr. du Progrès de la Somme, 1943.

Offers a dated analysis on prostitution in Amiens, but does include editions of useful primary documents on the subject.

359. Delcourt, Marie. *Hermaphrodite: Myths & Rites of the Bisexual Figure in Classical Antiquity*. London: Studio, 1961.

Maintains that women cross-dress primarily as a renunciation of and a rebellion against their families, established order and a sexual life.

360. Demurger, Alain. *Vie et mort de l'orde du Temple*. Paris: Le Seuil, 1985.

Provides a thorough history of the Knights Templars, and includes a chapter on their fall, the accusations, and the trial, including charges of homosexuality and sodomy.

361. Diepgen, Paul. *Frau und Frauenheilkunde in der Kultur des Mittelalters*. Stuttgart: G. Thieme, 1963.

362. Dillard, Heath. *Daughters of the Reconquest*. Cambridge: Cambridge University Press, 1985.

Studies Iberian town women between 1100-1300, and includes a discussion of prostitution and adultery.

363. Dinshaw, Carolyn. *Chaucer's Sexual Poetics*. Madison: University of Wisconsin Press, 1989.

Investigates the association between amatory acts and literary expressions in Chaucer's texts. Argues that gendered relations, such as courtship, marriage, and betrayal do not simply provide plot elements in Chaucer's works, but are central to an understanding of Chaucer's poetics and to the location of his poetry in a social context. Includes a discussion of *Troilus and Criseyde,* the *Legend of Good Women,* and the *Tales* of the Man of Law, Wife of Bath, the Clerk and the Pardoner.

364. Doherty, Dennis. *The Sexual Doctrine of Cardinal Cajetan*. Regensburg: Verlag Friedrich Pustet, 1966.

Analyzes the Cardinal's (and Thomas Aquinas') views on the sexual order, the abuses of sexuality, views on marriage, and many topics subsumed under these broad categories. Since Cardinal Cajetan wrote at the beginning of the 16th century, this book does not properly belong in a bibliography of the Middle Ages. However, I include it here because Cajetan was perhaps the most famous Thomist scholar and commentator, and his sexual doctrine may point the way through the Aquinas corpus and give medieval scholars a guide to Thomist thought. As Doherty writes, Cajetan "...is called not only a faithful interpreter of St. Thomas -- but his perfection." The book is scholarly and clear, and it is often difficult to achieve both in a work commenting on scholastic thought.

365. Dronke, Ursula. *The Role of Sexual Themes in Njal's Saga.* Dorothea Coke Memorial Lecture in Northern Studies, 1980. London: Viking Society for Northern Research, 1981.

Studies treatment and pattern of sexual experiences, emotions and attitudes in *Njal's Saga* (item 140), and argues that the author used sexual themes and motivations for "deepening the shallow image of human society" that the traditional saga conventions provided.

366. Duby, Georges, editor. *A History of Private Life: II Revelations of the Medieval World.* Translated by Arthur Goldhammer. Cambridge, MA: Harvard University Press, 1988.

Continues the study begun in volume one edited by Paul Veyne (item 521). Analyzes the concept and experience of private life in the Middle Ages from the eleventh through the fourteenth centuries. Within this broader discussion, which illuminates attitudes toward sexuality, the essays discuss marital intimacy, adultery, incest, homosexuality, and sodomy.

367. Dunning, Gerald C. *A Mediaeval Jug Found in London Decorated with Human and Animal Figures.* Paris: Private Publication, 1971.

Describes a jug with a figure of a naked woman with men and argues that the figure represents a prostitute from London's brothel area of Southwark.

368. Economous, Georges. *The Goddess Natura in Medieval Literature*. Cambridge, MA: Harvard University Press, 1972.

Focuses on the treatment of nature (and nature as sexuality) in Boetheus, Bernard Silvestiis, Alan of Lille, Jean de Meun and Chaucer.

369. Epton, Nina. *Love and the English.* New York: World Publishing Co., 1960.

Proposes to write a history of love in England from the Anglo-Saxons to the twentieth century. The section on the Middle Ages looks at evidence from Anglo-Saxon poetry through French romances translated into English, and recounts rumors of Norman homosexuality. An unscholarly account that contributes little.

370. ——. *Love and the French.* New York: World Publishing Co., 1959.

Purports to study the history of love in France from the troubadours of the twelfth century through the twentieth century. Discusses both courtly and erotic love, describes prostitution in France and retells romances that include accounts of rape and seduction. A descriptive rather than analytic account that frequently sounds like an historical novel, rather than a scholarly account.

371. Evans, G. R. *Alan of Lille: The Frontiers of Theology in the Later Twelfth Century*. Cambridge: Cambridge University Press, 1983.

Introduces Alan of Lille's thought. While this work does not deal solely with Alan of Lille's position on sin and sexuality, it provides comprehensive background on Alan and is helpful to use in conjunction with his works on sexuality.

372. Evans, W.F., ed. *Pseudo-Aristotle: The "Secret of Secrets."* London: Warburg Institute, 1982.

Offers a collection of well-chosen essays on this widely circulated medical text that discusses medical knowledge on sexuality.

373. Finke, Heinrich. *Papsttum und Untergang des Templerordens*. Münster: Aschendorff, 1907.

Appraises the accusations against the Templars, including accusations of sodomy. While an old study, it remains useful for its inclusion of materials from the Aragonese archives.

374. Flandrin, Jean Louis. *Un Temps pour Embrasser: aux origines de la morale sexuelle occidentale vie - xie siècle*. Paris: Seuil, 1983.

Studies the ideal of periodic continence, and how it assumed such a central place in church doctrine between the sixth and ninth centuries. Includes a discussion of fecundity, birth control, prohibitions on intercourse (i.e., during menstruation and on holy days). The author argues that before the seventh century, clerics were willing simply to preach in favor of periodic continence in marriage. After that, they imposed penances, so the prohibitions became more rigid. Perhaps the most interesting aspect of this work is the author's demonstration that most people did not accept these prohibitions without resistance.

375. ——. *Le Sexe et L'Occident*. Paris: Editions du Seuil, 1981.

Deals mostly with the early modern and modern periods, though Flandrin does at times discuss the Middle Ages as he looks at the origins of practices and attitudes (see especially the chapter, "Mariage tardif et vie sexuelle: discussions et hypotheses de recherche"). The work as a whole is invaluable for anyone interested in the history of sexuality for its theoretical approach to the study.

376. Fort, George F. *History of European Morals*. New York: George Braziller, 1955.

377. Foucault, Michel. *History of Sexuality* vol. 1. Translated by Robert Hurley. New York: Pantheon Books, 1978.

Does not deal directly with the Middle Ages, but offers a method for studying the history of sexuality by considering and challenging prevailing hypotheses about the nature of historical repression and the relationship between power-knowledge-pleasure that forms the core of sexual repression. An influential book that has shaped studies of sexuality.

378. Frantzen, Allen J. *The Literature of Penance in Anglo-Saxon England*. New Brunswick, NJ: Rutgers University Press, 1983.

Surveys penitential literature describing their origins in Ireland in the sixth century and the subsequent spread to England. This work covers until the tenth century. Mentions the penances for sexual sins, but this book should be supplemented by Payer's fuller treatment (item 468).

379. Fuchs, Eduard. *Das Erotische Element in der Karikatur*. Berlin: A. Hoffman & Co., 1904.

380. ——. *Geschichte der Erotischen Kunst in Einzeldarstellungen*. München: Albert Langen, 1923.

381. ——. *Illustrierte Sittengeschichte vom Mittelalter bis zur Gegenwart*. München: Albert Langen, 1909.

382. Fuchs, Eric. *Sexual Desire and Love: Origins and History of the Christian Ethic of Sexuality and Marriage*. Translated by M. Daigle. Cambridge: James Clark & Co., 1983.

Recapitulates scriptural Christian and patristic works on marriage and sex with the goal to "free" sexuality from old "oppressive" ideas. A satisfactory, though not remarkable, work.

383. Furber, D. *et al. Erotic Love in Literature from Medieval Legend to Romantic Illusion*. Troy, NY: Whitston Pub. Co., 1982.

Defines erotic love as that which is so overpowering that awareness of gender differences is lost, then proceeds to analyze some medieval literature in the light of this definition. This work is valuable only to the degree one accepts the initial definition.

384. Fyler, John M. *Chaucer and Ovid*. New Haven: Yale University Press, 1979.

385. Garde, Noel I. *Jonathan to Gide: The Homosexual in History*. New York: Vantage Press, 1964.

Presents a biographical dictionary of men throughout history who have "been referred to" as "being homosexual, of homoerotic temperament or of having had homosexual relations." This broad definition permits the author to include many people from Jesus to Pope John XXII to King Magnus the effeminate of Norway. Of, at best, dubious historical use.

386. Geremek, Bronislaw. *The Margins of Society in Late Medieval Paris.* Cambridge: Cambridge University Press, 1987.

Contains one section on prostitution in Paris from the thirteenth to the fifteenth centuries. Studies mainly judicial records, but supplements them with information from literary sources (fabliaux, poetry, and the *Roman de la Rose*) to describe the life of prostitutes. Includes information on regulations about where prostitutes may live and practice, sumptuary laws, pimps, and procuresses. The notes are an excellent guide to archival sources.

387. Gilson, Étienne. *Héloïse and Abélard.* Chicago: Henry Regnery Col, 1951.

Studies the famous relationship between Héloïse and Abélard, including her seduction and rape and his subsequent castration in terms of the philosophy expressed in their writings. A sensitive, and profound analysis by an undisputed master of medieval philosophy.

388. Gmelin, Julius. *Schuld oder Unschuld des Templerordens: Kritischer Versuch zur Lösung der Frage.* Stuttgart: W. Kohlhammer, 1893.

Argues that the Templars were innocent of all charges against them.

389. Goodich, Michael. *The Unmentionable Vice: Homosexuality in the Later Medieval Period*. Santa Barbara, CA: ABC Clio, Inc., 1979.

Examines the development of repression of homosexual acts through the late medieval period. Begins with the Gregorian Reform and ends with the thirteenth-century conciliar and legal developments. Focuses primarily on legal sources. The appendix contains a translation of the remarkably detailed trial of Arnold of Verniolle for sodomy and heresy. The book is well argued, balanced and a valuable piece of scholarship.

390. Gordon, B.L. *Medieval and Renaissance Medicine*. London: Peter Owen, 1959.

Argues unconvincingly for the existence of syphilis in medieval Europe. Compare with the contrary argument presented by Grmek, item 394.

391. Graham, James. *The Homosexual Kings of England*. London: Tandem, 1968.

Purports to describe the lives of English kings reputed to have been homosexual. It briefly discusses William Rufus, Richard I, Edward II, Richard II, James I and William III. The book lacks evidence to support its claims for historical events, presumes to know what the principals were thinking and feeling at moments in their lives, and searches for the source of their "deviance." A superficial work.

392. Graves, Roland J. *Flamenca: Variations sur les thèmes de l'amour courtois*. New York: Peter Lang, 1983.

Offers six essays on various topics related to the twelfth-century romance, *Flamenca*. Argues, without too much support, that the romance presents a new erotic sensibility.

393. Greenberg, David F. *The Construction of Homosexuality*. Chicago: University of Chicago Press, 1988.

Brings a sociological approach to the study of conceptions of and responses to homosexuality across cultures and across time to attempt to understand modern opinions. Disputes Boswell's contention (item 310) that increased urbanization coincided with acceptance of homosexual activity. Argues instead that social conceptions were more influential in shaping activity. Includes one chapter that considers "social responses to homosexuality in feudal societies," and continues the solid summary of medieval trends in a chapter that traces repression of homosexuality from the fourteenth century.

394. Grmek, Mirko Drazen. *Les Maladies à l'aube de la Civilisation Occidentale.* Paris: Payot, 1983.

Argues convincingly that syphilis was introduced to Europe after the Middle Ages.

395. Guttentag, M. and P. F. Secord. *Too Many Women? The Sex Ratio Question*. Beverly Hills, CA: Sage Publications, 1983.

Attempts to understand sexual patterns on the basis of a society's sex ratio. Thus the contrast between the early and the late Middle Ages regarding freedom of sexuality, misogyny and nascent feminism was attributed to the differing sex ratio between the two eras. Thought-provoking, but the evidence is selected too idiosyncratically.

396. Harvey, E.R. *The Inward Wits: Psychological Theory in the Middle Ages and Renaissance.* London: Warburg Institute, 1975.

Includes a discussion of obsessive sexual desire.

397. Hays, Hoffman Reynolds. *The Dangerous Sex: The Myth of Feminine Evil.* New York: G.P. Putnam's Sons, 1964.

Approaches historical and cross-cultural male attitudes towards women and argues that men's attitudes have shaped social organizations, and further that such attitudes arise from tensions (i.e., Oedipal) experienced by men. The sections on the Middle Ages cover the early Christians, courtly love, Boccaccio and Chaucer. While not a scholarly work, it is a sensitive, perceptive analysis.

398. Healy, Emma Therese. *Women According to Saint Bonaventure*. New York: Georgian Press, 1955.

399. Heaney, S.P. *The Development of the Sacramentality of Marriage from Anselm of Laon to Thomas Aquinas*. Washington, D.C.: Catholic University of America Press, 1963.

Weaves considerations of intercourse throughout this solid discussion of the development of the growth of the idea of marriage as a sacrament during the golden years of scholastic thought.

400. Heinsohn, Gunnar and Otto Steiger. *Die Vernichtung der Weisen Frauen*. Herbstein: Marz, 1985.

Develops further the argument he articulated in his article, "Elimination of Medieval Birth Control," item 640.

401. Helmholz, Richard H. *Marriage Litigation in Medieval England*. Cambridge: Cambridge University Press, 1974.

Presents a concise and useful description of marriage litigation in England from the late thirteenth to the end of the fifteenth centuries. It includes a section describing litigation to secure divorce on the grounds of male impotence, and the evidence necessary to pursue such a claim.

402. Hewson, M. Anthony. *Giles of Rome and the Medieval Theory of Conception*. London: The Athlone Press, 1975.

Contributes an excellent summary and analysis of Giles' work that is comprehensible to non-specialists. This is a good introduction to medieval reproduction theory. Giles was a thirteenth-century schoolman who wrote *De formatione corporis humani in utero* that provided a review of existing medical knowledge and contributed to philosophical and medical embryological theories.

403. Hexter, Ralph. *Ovid and Medieval Schooling*. München: Bei der Arbeo-Gesellschaft, 1986.

Studies medieval school commentaries on Ovid's *Ars Amatoria, Epistulae ex Ponto,* and *Epistulae Heroidum* looking in detail at the glosses, language, allegorizing, and other elements. Notes that the Medieval commentators did not try to suppress Ovid's open discussions of sexual intercourse, but did try to explain away Ovid's homosexual references. The commentators provide a window into medieval attitudes as they studied classic texts.

404. Himes, Norman Edwin. *Medical History of Contraception.* New York: Gamut Press, Inc., 1963.

Includes one chapter on contraceptive practices in the medieval West, focusing on Islamic medicine, and the medieval schoolmen. Concludes that medieval contraceptive use was not widespread, a conclusion challenged by more recent work.

405. Huchet, J. *L'Amour Discourtois - La "Fin'Amors" chez les premiers troubadours.* Toulouse: Privat, 1987.

406. Hunt, Morton M. *The Natural History of Love.* New York: Alfred A. Knopf, 1959.

Outlines the history of sexuality from the classical period to the twentieth century. The three chapters on the Middle Ages focus on patristics, courtly love and witchcraft. The work is readable, but neither comprehensive nor sophisticated.

407. Irsigler, Franz, and Arnold Lassotta. *Better und Gaukles, Dirnen und Henkei: Randgruppen und Aussenseiter in Köln 1300-1600.* Köln: Greven Verlag, 1984.

408. Jacquart, Danielle, and Claude Thomasset. *Sexuality and Medicine in the Middle Ages.* Translated by Matthew Adamson. Princeton: Princeton University Press, 1988.

Analyzes comprehensively medieval medical tracts that deal with sexuality. Offers an in-depth study of medieval perceptions of anatomy, physiology, medicine, and venereal disease. In addition, the authors place medical wisdom in the context of other aspects of medieval thought, such as courtly love and theology. Among other suggestive themes, explains the connection between medicine and misogyny, describes the thirteenth-century introduction of Arabic erotica into the West, and maintains that the courtly love tradition advocated *coitus interruptus* as the ideal form of safe intercourse. This will remain an important book not only for its well-argued theses, but as an introduction to the medical sources on sexuality.

409. Janson, H.W. *Apes and Ape Lore in the Middle Ages and the Renaissance*. London: Warburg Institute, 1952.

Explores thoroughly the ape motif in late medieval art. The ape was a symbol of female sexuality and wantonness (in contrast with the bear of male sexuality). The use of the symbols can shed light on medieval perceptions of sexuality.

410. Johansson, Warren, et al. *Homosexuality, Intolerance and Christianity*. New York: Scholarship Committee, 1981.

Reviews the criticisms of Boswell's influential book on homosexuality, item 310.

411. Johnson, David J. *Southwark and the City*. Oxford: Oxford University Press, 1969.

Provides a carefully documented history of the Borough of Southwark, near London, from the fourteenth to the twentieth centuries. Bankside in Southwark was the brothel area of London throughout the Middle Ages, so this work provides a full context for a study of prostitution in Britain.

412. Jones, Rosemarie. *The Theme of Love in the Romans d'Antiquité*. London: Modern Humanities Research Association, 1972.

Attempts to analyze the way in which love themes (both "Ovidian" and "courtly") have been treated in the group of romances that deal with classical antiquity (*Thebes*, *Eneas*, *Troie* and *Alexander*, and the poems of *Pyramus et Thebes* and *Narcissus*). The analysis is not sufficient to provide more than a superficial introduction to the works.

413. Karlen, Arno. *Sexuality and Homosexuality.* New York: Norton, 1971.

Contains two chapters on the Middle Ages, which are both either too general or selectively anecdotal. Both extremes make this work not helpful to serious scholars. Contains an extensive bibliography, but no notes.

414. Karnein, Alfred. *De Amore in Volkssprachlicher Literatur*. Heidelberg: Carl Winter Universitätsverlag, 1985.

Examines various interpretations of Andreas Capellanus' treatise "De Amore" from the twelfth century through the Renaissance. The author believes that Andreas' work represents the desire to free sexuality from the hostility of the educated clergy. This is an objective, scholarly work with an extensive bibliography. While it may not solve all the controversies surrounding Andreas' treatise, it makes a sound contribution to the debate.

415. Kelly, Henry Ansgar. *Love and Marriage in the Age of Chaucer*. Ithaca: Cornell University Press, 1975.

Considers Chaucer's works and analyzes what values and practices of love, marriage and sex the authors expressed. This work goes beyond the literary evidence to describe the canon lawyers' and theologians' views on the same subjects. An excellent piece of scholarship.

416. Kelly, Walter Keating. *Curiosities of Indo-European Tradition and Folk-lore* London:. Chapman & Hall, 1863.

Describes the worship of Fryg as a fertility symbol in Medieval England and Belgium. Although the work is dated, it offers some useful insights.

417. Kerns, Joseph E. *The Theology of Marriage.* New York: Sheed and Ward, Inc., 1964.

Surveys biblical, patristic and medieval thought on such topics as the nature of marriage, original sin and sexual desire, and concludes that marriage is within God's plan and that sexual desire, while not completely sinful, must be used with restraint. This is not an in-depth analysis of medieval attitudes, but primarily a collection of quotations that attempts to prove its point by preponderance of evidence rather than hard analysis. Too superficial for the serious scholar, and has been superceded by later works (see particularly Peter Brown, item 321, and James Brundage, item 323).

418. Kuhn, Adalbert. *Die Herabkunft des Feuers und des Göttertranks*. Berlin: Ferdinand Dümmler's Verlagsbuchhandlung, 1859.

Presents a romanticized view of Indoeuropean mythology, which includes, among other things, a description of Scottish phallic ceremonies at Inverkeithing.

419. Labarge, Margaret Wade. *A Small Sound of the Trumpet: Women in Medieval Life*. Boston: Beacon Press, 1986.

Includes a chapter on "Women on the Fringe" which contains a general (albeit well-supported) discussion on medieval prostitutes, particularly in France and England.

420. LaCroix, Paul. *Histoire de la Prostitution Chez Tous les Peuples du Monde depuis l'Antiquité la Plus Reculée jusqu'à nos Jours*. 6 vols. Brussels: Rozez, 1851-53.

Offers an analysis too dated to be useful, but the text refers comprehensively to editions of sources.

421. Ladurie, Emmanuel LeRoy. *Montaillou: The Promised Land of Error.* Translated by Barbara Bray. New York: Vintage Books, 1979.

Uses the inquisition records of Jacques Fournier (item 196) to recreate life in a fourteenth-century village of southern France. Includes a description of the sexual life and attitudes of the village, including homosexuality, prostitution, and rape.

422. Laeuchli, Samuel. *Power and Sexuality. The Emergence of Canon Law at the Synod of Elvira*. Philadelphia: Temple University Press, 1972.

Summarizes the canons of the Council of Elvira in mid-fourth century Spain that regulate sexuality. Laeuchli sees the legislation as necessary for a church beginning to establish its power.

423. Laurent, Emile and Paul Nagaur. *Magica Sexualis*. New York: Anthropological Press, 1934.

Purports to be a scholarly work exploring the history of such practices as sexual black masses, aphrodisiacs and other sexual magic. Instead, it is a compendium of sexual stories intended to titillate. It fails both as erotica and scholarship.

424. Lecky, W.E.H. *History of European Morals from Augustus to Charlemagne*. New York: Braziller, 1955.

Reprints a nineteenth-century work, and includes a discussion on sexuality, rape and prostitution. The work is dated, biased and the conclusions ill supported.

425. Leclercq, Jean. *Monks on Marriage: A Twelfth Century View*. New York: Seabury Press, 1982.

Studies marital love as discussed by some twelfth-century monks and regular canons. Shows that twelfth-century thinkers and hagiographic models stressed the importance of love in marriage. Leclercq also discusses prostitution and attitudes toward it. A fine sensitive work.

426. Legman, Gershon. *The Guilt of the Templars*. New York: Basic Books, 1966.

Contains four essays on the guilt of the Templars. The introductory essay by Legman argues that the Templars were guilty of most of the charges against them, including homosexual practices. Another essay by Thomas Wright argues that the Templars represented one example of phallic worship that was common throughout the Middle Ages. Neither article is particularly convincing.

427. LeGoff, Jacques. *The Medieval Imagination*. Translated by Arthur Goldhammer. Chicago: University of Chicago Press, 1988.

Contains item 684.

428. Lehmann, Andrée. *Le Rôle de la Femme dans l'Histoire de France au Moyen Age*. Paris: Berger-Levrault, 1952.

Includes a discussion of prostitution.

429. Lehmann, Paul. *Die Parodie im Mittelalter*. München: Drei Masken Verlag, 1922.

Studies the use of parody in the Middle Ages and traces its roots from classical literature. The sources used for the discussion were primarily poetic, and the humor often focused on clerical sexual and licentious behavior. Also analyzes grammar as a sexual metaphor. This work directs the reader to the literary sources, and provides editions of poems containing sexual humor in the supplementary volume.

430. Leibbrand, A. *Formen des Eros*. Freiburg/München: Verlag Karl Alber, 1972.

Traces the development of views of sexuality from the ancient world to the Middle Ages, showing the influence of Germanic and classical beliefs on Christian society. Focuses primarily on central Europe, and surveys a full range of sexual beliefs and practices. An objective and thorough survey.

431. Lenient, Charles Félix. *La Satire en France au Moyen Age*. Paris: Hachette, 1877.

432. Lerner, Robert E. *The Heresy of the Free Spirit in the Later Middle Ages*. Berkeley: University of California Press, 1972.

Asserts that the Free Spirit heresy that has the reputation of antinomian licentiousness was actually a movement of pious mysticism without the sexual freedom attributed to it. In the course of this argument, the author provides a number of references to the heretics' reputed sexual excesses, thus the book gives valuable insights into some attitudes toward sexuality regardless of whether followers of the Free Spirit practiced them or not.

433. Lewinsohn, Richard. *A History of Sexual Customs*. New York: Harper & Bros., 1958.

Traces the history of sexual customs from prehistory through the twentieth century. Contains chapters on Christianity, in which he associates Christianity with sexual repression and population decline, Islam, and the development of erotic literature, and the Middle Ages, describing troubadour poetry, prostitution, and the affair of Abélard and Héloïse. General and superficial.

434. Lo Duca, Giuseppe. *Histoire de L'Érotisme*. Paris: Jean-Jacques Pauvert, 1954.

Reviews briefly the history of eroticism from prehistory through the early twentieth century. Purports to introduce a scientific study of eroticism (from which the author excludes pornography) as a broader category of the study of "sexology." Argues that sexology studies sexuality as a branch of biology, while eroticism includes the social, cultural, and psychological dimensions of sexuality. Includes one chapter on the Middle Ages (titled the "Christian Epochs"). Argues that this was an era of sexual repression in which eroticism was expressed in witchcraft and courtly love. The work contains many illustrations.

435. Löffler, Josef. *Die Störungen des geschlechtlichen Vermögens in der Literatur der autoritativen Theologie des Mittelalters*. Mainz: Akademie der Wissenschaften, 1958.

Discusses impotence in the Middle Ages and its treatment by doctors, theologians and canon lawyers.

436. Longworth, T. Clifton. *The Devil a Monk would be: A Survey of Sex and Celibacy in Religion*. London: H. Joseph, Ltd., 1936.

Describes erotic symbols in medieval churches that depict prostitution, homosexuality, masturbation, and general erotic scenes. Argues that the presence of such images was due to the rule of clerical celibacy. The whole work is a strong polemic against clerical celibacy, and sees the Reformation as having introduced a new healthy attitude into a decadent world.

437. Lorcin, Maria-Thérèse. *Façons de Sentir et de Penser: Les Fabliaux Français.* Paris: H. Champion, 1979.

Studies certain themes that emerge from the fabliaux, including the treatment of fornication, prostitution and even notes the presence of gigolos. This is an unusual approach to the texts, and provides a refreshing perspective.

438. Lucie-Smith, Edward. *Eroticism in Western Art.* London: Thames and Hudson, 1972.

Analyzes eroticism in church carvings. Even in his chapter on the Middle Ages, however, his primary focus is on early Renaissance materials.

439. Lufti al-Sayyid-Marsont, Afaf, editor. *Society and the Sexes in Medieval Islam.* Malibu, CA: Undena Publications, 1979.

Collects seven essays on various topics on sexuality in medieval Islam. Within discussions of sources ranging from literature and law to letters, includes analyses of bestiality, homosexuality, incest, sodomy, masturbation, and adultery. All the essays are insightful works that both stand on their own and point to further research on the topics. A fine collection.

440. Luria, Maxwell. *A Reader's Guide to the* Roman de la Rose. Hamden, CT: Archon Books, 1982.

Provides a full bibliography and discussion of topics such as manuscripts traditions. Includes a summary of the work and lists of personifications and allusions.

441. Maclagan, Robert Craig. *Scottish Myths. Notes on Scottish History & Tradition.* Edinburgh: Maclachlen & Stewart, 1882.

Analyzes Scottish myths, and includes descriptions of phallic worship and imagery.

442. Manselli, R. *Famille et Parente dans l'Occident Médiéval*. Ecole Française de Rome: Palais Farnese, 1977.

Analyzes the kinds of incest mentioned in the penitentials.

443. Martin, Edward J. *The Trial of the Templars*. London: George Allen & Unwin, 1928.

Offers a statistical analysis of some of the confessions, determining the percentage that confessed to obscene kissing, sexual licence, etc.

444. Martines, Lauro, editor. *Violence and Civil Disorder in Italian Cities 1200-1500*. Berkeley: University of California Press, 1972.

Contains items 562 and 641.

445. Masters, R. E. L. *Eros and Evil: The Sexual Psychopathology of Witchcraft*. New York: Julian Press, Inc., 1962.

Examines the belief that it is possible to have intercourse with demons, which prevailed from the twelfth through the seventeenth centuries. Includes descriptions of the nature of intercourse, demons' semen and offspring of human/demon relationships. Masters concludes with the fairly obvious observation that these perceptions were results of psychotic delusions. This book contains one of the fullest descriptions of this phenomenon, but unfortunately the casual use of citations impedes its use as a scholarly tool.

446. Mausbach, Joseph. *Die Ethik des hl. Augustinus* 2 vol. Freiburg: Herder & Co., 1929.

447. Mayhew, Henry. *London Labour and the London Poor*. 2 vols. New York: Harper, 1851.

Includes a discussion of prostitution, but the material is dated.

448. McCall, Andrew. *The Medieval Underworld*. North Pomfret, VT: Hamish Hamilton, 1979.

Contributes a general analysis of medieval "outsiders," and includes one chapter on prostitutes and one on homosexuals. The limited space precludes detailed information, yet the sources are well used and this makes a good introductory work.

449. Ménard, Philippe. *Les Fabliaux: Contes à Rire du Moyen Age*. Paris: Presses Universitaires de France, 1983.

450. Mercier, Vivian. *The Irish Comic Tradition*. Oxford: Oxford University Press, 1962.

Describes early Irish portrayals of the sexually grotesque in art (both phallic figures and female figures with exaggerated genitalia) and argues that the sexual symbols in Ireland always associate sex with death. A general discussion that ranges from the ninth century to the present. The argument for the Middle Ages is not very convincing.

451. Murphy, Emmett. *Great Bordellos of the World*. New York: Quartet Books, 1983.

Presents an illustrated history of houses of prostitution. Its two chapters on the Middle Ages are not very satisfactory, and anyone looking for specific information on medieval prostitution should look elsewhere.

452. Murray, Margaret Alice. *The Witch Cult in Western Europe*. Oxford: Clarendon Press, 1921.

Stresses the reputed sexual practices of witches by accepting the Inquisition records at face value. More sensational than scholarly.

453. Musallam, B.F. *Sex and Society in Islam: Birth Control Before the Nineteenth Century*. Cambridge: Cambridge University Press, 1983.

Includes information on the Middle Ages, including a discussion of the widely influential Avicenna.

454. Muscatine, Charles. *The Old French Fabliaux*. New Haven: Yale University Press, 1986.

Maintains that the sexual references in the fabliaux would not have shocked the medieval audience, who was used to an open sexuality. A solid, general work on the French fabliaux that will surely remain a central work on the subject. Muscatine's use of the fabliaux as historical windows into past attitudes should be contrasted with Howard Bloch, item 307, who sees the tales as psychological, not necessarily historical.

455. Newman, Barbara. *Sister of Wisdom: St. Hildegard's Theology of the Feminine*. Berkeley: University of California Press, 1987.

Approaches the thought of Hildegard from the point of view of a theologian, and argues that although in her medical writings, Hildegard treated female sexuality in a relatively positive light, in her theological tract she claimed that grace is dependent upon a renunciation of sexuality.

456. Noble, H.D. *Les Passions dans la Vie Morale, 2 vol.* Paris: Lethielleux, 1931.

Offers a theological analysis of how one can live a moral life in spite of the passions that assail, and uses the theology (and psychology) of Thomas Aquinas to explicate this theme. The author only includes modern writers to verify Thomistic thought. Volume 1 discusses the passions from the point of view of psychology, and volume 2 considers the morality of passions. The analysis includes the passion of concupiscence and considers the nature of "passionate movements" outside the realm of reason.

457. Noonan, John T. Jr. *Contraception: A History of Its Treatment by the Catholic Theologians*. Cambridge, Mass.: Harvard University Press, 1986.

Surveys contraception, both the growth of the concept and the development of the practice from the Roman Empire through 1965. A comprehensive study.

458. Nykrog, Per. *Les Fabliaux Librairie*. Geneva: Droz, 1973.

Provides one of the best discussions of the origins and purposes of these comic, often bawdy, stories available, and a necessary starting point for anyone using these works. He includes in his discussion an analysis of the erotic tales, the use of obscenity in the stories, the use of parody and other issues of equal importance in beginning to understand the expressions of sexuality in these tales. Contains an extensive bibliography.

459. O'Faolain, Julia. *Not in God's Image*. New York: Harper & Row, 1973.

Collects extracts from primary sources about women. Includes a chapter on the Early Middle Ages, which provides references to Germanic law codes that refer to adultery and rape, and chapters that include some information on medicine and childbearing. The whole book suffers from a malady that frequently plagues collections - selections idiosyncratically chosen, short and out of context can be deceiving.

460. Otis, Leah Lydia. *Prostitution in Medieval Society*. Chicago: University of Chicago Press, 1985.

Describes the regularization and organization of prostitutes in Southern France in the late Middle Ages during which prostitution became authorized and controlled. Argues that prostitution was tolerated before the twelfth century, institutionalized in the thirteenth and fourteenth centuries, and only repressed later. Provides a well-documented study that should prove a model for future such studies, and contains a comprehensive bibliography.

461. Pagels, Elaine. *Adam, Eve, and the Serpent*. New York: Random House, 1988.

Explores the development of sexual attitudes in the Christian tradition that derived from interpretations of Genesis. Contains some of Augustine's views of sexuality, but focuses mostly on questions of freedom and free will.

462. Pansier, Pierre. *L'Oeuvre des Repenties à Avignon du XIIIe au XVIII siècle.* Paris: H. Champion, 1910.

Includes within a general discussion of penitents in Avignon editions of documents useful for a study of prostitution.

463. Parent-Duchatelet, Alexander. *De la Prostitution dans la Ville de Paris.* 2 vols. New York: H. Baillière, 1857.

464. Parrinder, Edward Jeffrey. *Sex and the World's Religions*. New York: Oxford University Press, 1980.

Contains one chapter devoted to Christian diversity that includes Greco-Roman, Judaic and medieval treatment of sex and homosexuality. In its brevity, it is superficial and misleading.

465. Partner, Peter. *The Murdered Magicians: The Templars and Their Myth*. London: Oxford University Press, 1982.

Contributes a thorough and balanced account of the fall of the Templars and their trial. Discusses the probable validity of the charges of heresy and sodomy that were brought against the Templars. One of the significant contributions of this book is to analyze the growth of the myth of the Templars as magicians.

466. Partridge, B. *A History of Orgies*. New York: Crown Publishers, 1960.

Studies "orgies" defined as sexually rebellious behavior of various kinds from the ancient Greeks to the 20th century. The chapter on the Middle Ages alternates between being too general to be informative and too inaccurate to be useful. Even the reader with casual interest would do better to look elsewhere.

467. Payen, Jean Charles. *La Rose et l'Utopie: Révolution sexuelle et communisme nostalgique chez Jean de Meung*. Paris: Editions Sociales, 1976.

Claims that in the *Roman de la Rose*, Jean de Meun advocates a utopia that provides for communism and sexual liberation.

468. Payer, Pierre J. *Sex and the Penitentials*. Toronto: University of Toronto Press, 1984.

Investigates the regulation of sexual behavior in the penitentials from 550-1150. Among other topics, covers rules concerning heterosexual acts, homosexuality, bestiality,and masturbation. A scholarly analysis.

469. Perella, N.J. *The Kiss Sacred and Profane*. Berkeley: University of California Press, 1969.

Analyzes the kiss as used in the religious and secular literature from early Christianity through the Renaissance. Studies the kiss as a union of breath (and soul), as a prelude to and promise of further sexual activity, and as simple sensual pleasure. For the secular works, he studies the Troubadour poetry, *Carmina Burana,* and some French romances. A fine introduction to a subject that can shed light on sexual attitudes.

470. Perez-Rioja, José António. *El Amor en la Literatura*. Madrid: Editorial Tecnos, S.A., 1983.

Offers a wide-ranging and general discussion on love in literature (mainly Spanish, but it does occasionally depart from the Spanish material) from the ancient world through the twentieth century. Provides a breakdown of "types" of lovers and women in the Middle Ages, including prostitutes, adulterers, etc. While it is a good general introduction to the subject, it is too broad to be of use to more than the generalist.

471. Pfeffer, Wendy. *The Change of Philomel: The Nightingale in Medieval Literature*. New York: Peter Lang, 1985.

Recounts the medieval instances of the image of the nightingale, symbol of love in a variety of literary genres. See especially Chapter 7, "Sex and the Single Nightingale" which discusses the bird's symbol of both male and female sexuality. It is a good guide for those who would trace this symbolic use of sexuality, but this book does contain some errors of translation and usage so it must be used carefully.

472. Philippson, Ernst Alfred. *Germanisches Heidenthum bei den Angelsachsen.* Leipzig: Verlag von Bern. Tauchnitz, 1929.

473. Pierrugues, Pierre. *Glossarium eroticum linguae latinae sive theogoniae, legum et morum nuptialium apud Romanos....* Amsterdam: Adolf M. Hakkert, 1965.

Provides a useful reference work.

474. Poirion, Daniel. *Le Roman de la Rose*. Paris: Hatier, 1973.

Contributes a thorough study of the *Roman de la Rose*.

475. Rabutaux, M. *De la Prostitution en Europe depuis l'Antiquité jusqu'à le fin de l'XVI siècle.* Paris: Duquesne, 1869.

Reproduces a number of primary sources dealing with prostitution which are useful even though the total analysis is dated.

476. Raby, F.J.E. *A History of Secular Latin Poetry in the Middle Ages*. Oxford: Clarendon Press, 1934.

Presents a comprehensive survey of medieval secular Latin poetry. While the direct treatment of erotic subjects within the verses is disappointingly absent, the work helps explain the literature and its context. The author also directs the reader to some of the erotic works, such as the story of *Lantfrid* and *Cobbo* (from the Cambridge songs), the French *Comoedia,* the erotic poems of the Ripoll manuscript and, of course, the *Carmina Burana* and the Archpoet. For these reasons, the book is worth including here and worth consulting for those exploring sexuality within the poetic literature.

477. Radcliff-Umstead, Douglas, editor. *Human Sexuality in the Middle Ages and Renaissance*. Pittsburgh: University of Pittsburgh Press, 1978.

Collects essays on various sexual themes. There are several of interest to medievalists: Dorothy S. McCoy discusses the story of Robert the Devil (an old French fabliau), Douglas Radcliff-Umstead on erotic sin in the *Divine Comedy*, and perhaps most enlightening, a scholarly summary of medical perceptions of sexuality by Thomas G. Benedek, which includes a description of aphrodisiacs, anaphrodisiacs, and abortives.

478. Randall, Lilian M.C. *Images in the Margins of Gothic Manuscripts*. Berkeley: University of California Press, 1966.

Describes a collection of marginalia of Gothic manuscripts. It is well indexed with an excellent bibliography, and illustrates intercourse, voyeurism and scatological themes.

479. Rank, O. *Das Inzest Motiv in Dichtung und Sage*. Darmstadt: Wissenschaftliche Buchgesellschaft, 1974.

Uses Freudian analysis to uncover largely hidden incest themes in ancient myths, fables and fairy tales. This is reprinted from a 1926 revision of a 1212 work. It is too dated in its methodology and too imprecise in its scholarship.

480. Rey-Flaud, H. *La Névrose Courtoise*. Paris: Navarin, Editeur, 1983.

481. Richard, Guy. *Histoire de L'Amour en France*. Paris: J-C Lattes, 1985.

Intends to be a general summary of the subject from the Middle Ages to the twentieth century. It focuses mainly on the fabliaux for the medieval material. The whole work is drawn from a few secondary sources (albeit solid ones), and is not for a scholarly audience.

482. Robert, Ulysse. *Les Signes d'Infamie au Moyen Âge: Juifs, Sarrasins, Hérétiques, Lépreux, Cagots et Filles Publiques*. Paris: H. Champion, 1891.

Offers a brief summary of legislation showing that in the thirteenth century certain groups were required to wear special articles of clothing to demonstrate their identity. One chapter is devoted to clothing prostitutes are required to wear.

483. Robinson, Victor. *Encyclopedia Sexualis: A Comprehensive Encyclopedia-Dictionary of the Sexual Sciences*. New York: Dingwell-Rock, Ltd., 1936.

Provides an alphabetical listing of sexual terms, and the narrative that accompanies each term often includes historical data (for example, for the Middle Ages, see "Chastity Belt"). The historical material should be used cautiously; in an effort to avoid bowdlerism, the authors moved toward sensationalism.

484. Roselló Vaquer, Ramón. *L'homosexualitat a Mallorca a la edat Mitjana*. Barcelona: Olaneta, 1978.

Reviews trial records and sentences in the royal archives of Mallorca and presents excerpts that show executions for homosexuality, sodomy, and bestiality in the fifteenth and sixteenth centuries. Includes an appendix on other sexual "crimes" mentioned in the archives -- transvestism, adultery, and prostitution. Based on this information, concludes prematurely that homosexuality was repressed throughout the Middle Ages, however, the data presented is informative. Unfortunately the quotations are not documented, so it would be difficult for scholars to find the original references. The publication is a short work written in Catalan.

485. Rossiaud, Jacques. *Medieval Prostitution*. Translated by Lydia G. Cochrane. New York: Basil Blackwell, 1988.

Analyzes the history of prostitution primarily in France from ca. 1300 to 1600, with emphasis on the fifteenth and sixteenth centuries. Demonstrates that prostitution was an accepted dimension of medieval society, and was suppressed in the sixteenth century. Contains a sensitive and perceptive study of gang rape, and women driven into prostitution as a result. A well researched and well developed work. Contains two appendices: one studying the Quarrel of the *Roman de la Rose,* (see item 130) and the other offering editions of documents on the history of prostitution.

486. Rousselle, Aline. *Porneia: On Desire and the Body in Antiquity*. Translated by Felicia Pheasant. Oxford: Basil Blackwell, 1988.

Studies pagan and Christian attitudes toward sexuality, desire and the body in a book of fascinating detail and sound scholarship. Discusses perceptions of the bodies of men, women, and children, drawing from evidence of medical texts, then considers the relationship between individuals, looking at laws of adultery, concubinage, divorce and prostitution. Includes an analysis of sacrifice during the Empire, which offers a discussion of castration which is insightful and surprising. Finally maintains that the social/intellectual context of classical male aversion to women and the social/legal condition of Roman women combined with an ascetic confrontation with desire in the Egyptian desert to create a Christianity that encouraged chastity or frigidity.

487. Rowland, Beryl. *Animals with Human Faces: A Guide to Animal Symbolism*. Knoxville: University of Tennessee Press, 1973.

Summarizes perceptions of animals taken from medieval bestiaries, and includes most of the symbolism available on each animal. Included in the discussion are the beliefs about the sexuality of many of the animals, and how these attributes are applied to humans. See, for example, the camel or the dog. Thus, the work guides one through the often bewildering medieval symbolism to some medieval attitudes on sexuality.

488. Rowse, A.L. *Homosexuals in History: A Study of Ambivalence in Society, Literature and the Arts*. New York: Macmillan Pub. Co., Inc. 1977.

Contains one chapter on the Middle Ages, which is both superficial and inaccurate. Anyone interested in the subject of homosexuality in the Middle Ages should not be misled by the title of this work into thinking that there might be useful information here, for there is none.

489. Roy, Bruno, editor. *L'Erotisme au Moyen Age*. Paris: Montparnasse, 1977.

Presents a collection of short essays that includes such topics as the sexual customs surrounding consummation of marriage and courting festivals, sexuality in music, and sodomy in medieval canon law. The essays are thought-provoking, although rather general.

490. Ruhe, Doris. *Le Dieu D'Amours avec son Paradis*. Munchen: Wilhelm Fink Verlag, 1974.

Considers the evolution of the God 'Amor' from the fourth to the fourteenth century, showing that Amor was at first tied closely to Venus, his mother. In time, Amor became separated from Venus, leaving Venus as the sexual side of love while Amor became powerful in his own right, yet divorced from carnal sexuality. Provides a good theoretical background for the study of the carnal. This work is written in German.

491. Ryan, John Joseph. *Saint Peter Damiani and his Canonical Sources*. Toronto: Pontificium Institutum Studiorum Mediae Aetatis, 1956.

Traces the precedents of church sexual legislation that was used during the Gregorian reform of the eleventh century.

492. Sabatier. *Histoire de la Législation sur les Femmes Publiques et les Lieux de Débauche*. Paris: J.P. Roret, 1828.

Studies prostitution in France based on police records.

493. Sacchi, Dott. *Della Condizione Economica, Morale e Politica degli Italiani ne' tempi Mun*. Milan: Presso Ant. Fort. Stella e Fig, 1829.

Contains an interesting description of a phallic procession at Pavia ca. 1350.

494. Salisbury, Joyce E. *Church Fathers, Independent Virgins*. London: Verso, 1990.

Looks at early Christian attitudes toward sexuality and considers how those attitudes shaped perceptions of women and rules for celibate women. The first half of the book explores two patristic views, first the view of the early fathers (mainly Tertullian, Jerome and Ambrose), and second the dramatic change in perceptions of sexuality introduced by Augustine. The second half of the book looks at an ascetic view of sexuality and virginity, that reveals a positive view of sexuality and women's bodies that is absent from the patristic works. It concludes that modern arguments that claim people trade their sexuality for personal freedom are not new, but have a tradition that goes back to the early Middle Ages.

495. Salusbury, G.T. *Street Life in Medieval England*. Oxford: Pen-In Hand, 1948.

496. Sanger, William. *A History of Prostitution*. New York: Harper & Bros., 1858.

Attempts a monumental study of prostitution throughout the world from earliest times through the nineteenth century. Contains chapters on the early Christian era, and France and Great Britain during the Middle Ages. Also includes a discussion of venereal diseases, which more recent studies have rendered obsolete. On the whole, the work was pathbreaking, but is now too general.

497. Saville, Jonathan. *The Medieval Erotic Alba: Structure as Meaning*. New York: Columbia University Press, 1972.

Studies a particular form of medieval poetry, the one in which a knight and lady are forced to separate from their adulterous liaison by the coming of dawn. This is a thorough and sensitive analysis pointing out the analogies to other aspects of medieval life, and the symbolic structure critical to the genre. While this book does not deal explicitly with sexuality, it introduces a medieval genre that deals explicitly with adultery.

498. Schlosser, F. *Andreas Capellanus: Seine Minnelehre und das christliche Weltbild um 1200.* Bonn: H. Bouvier, 1980.

499. Schöllgen, G. *Ecclesia sordida? Zur Frage der sozialen Schichtung Frühchristlicher Gemeinden am Beispiel Kartagos zur Zeit Tertullians.* Jahrbuch für Antike und Christetum: Ergänzungsband 12. Münster-inWestfalen: Aschendorff, 1984.

500. Shapiro, Marianne. *Women Earthly and Divine in the "Comedy" of Dante*. Lexington: University of Kentucky Press, 1975.

Contains a section on "lovers," which presents Dante's view of sexuality, particularly as applied to women. Argues that for Dante, active and sexual women were destructive for men.

501. Sheehan, Michael M. *Family and Marriage in Medieval Europe: A Working Bibliography*. Toronto: Medieval Studies Committee 1984.

Includes a section on attitudes to sexuality within a larger bibliography on topics in family, marriage, women, children, and other aspects of social history.

502. Sheridan, R. and Anne Ross. *Grotesque and Gargoyles: Paganism in the Medieval Church*. Newton Abbot: David & Charles Ltd., 1975.

Studies the "frankly sexual" carvings on churches, which include women exposing their genitals, men exposing anuses, and hermaphrodites. The work does not offer a convincing explanation for the appearance of these figures, merely offering some suggestions: fertility figures, warnings against sensuality or "evil-averting acts."

503. Simon, Edith. *The Piebald Standard: A Biography of the Knights Templars.* Boston: Little, Brown, 1959.

Includes a useful summary of the charges against the Templars.

504. Simons, G.L. *A Place for Pleasure: the History of the Brothel*. London: Harwood-Smart Publishing, 1975.

Surveys a large topic in a short work. Covers from ancient Greece to the twentieth century, but provides interesting and precise details. Framing the medieval information within a larger context yields a helpful introduction to the subject.

505. Siraisi, Nancy G. *The Canon and Medical Teaching in Italian Universities after 1500.* Princeton: Princeton University Press, 1987.

Deals mostly with the Renaissance tradition of Avicenna's influential medical work, but contains a summary of the medieval tradition.

506. Sorensen, P.M. *The Unmanly Man: Concepts of Sexual Defamation in Early Northern Society*. Translated by Joan Turville-Petre. Odense: Odense University Press, 1983.

Contributes a sophisticated and fascinating discussion of the legal and literary prevalence of sexual insults (whether verbal or physical) in old Scandinavian literature, and shows the importance of the concept of active masculinity in that society. This work is also a source of information for locating sexual references in the Sagas.

507. Spence, James Lewis. *The Mysteries of Britain*. London: Rider & Co., 1928.

Presents a dated and romanticized view of British religious rituals, including fertility rites.

508. Ström, Folke. *Nith, Ergi and Old Norse Moral Attitudes.* The Dorothea Coke Memorial Lecture in Northern Studies, 1974. London: The Viking Society for Northern Research, 1974.

Argues that *nith* refers to passive male homosexuality, and that it is a cultural paradigm for the broader concept of *ergi*, meaning unmanliness in general.

509. Tabori, Paul. *Social History of Rape*. London: New English Library, 1971.

Argues that rape is an integral part of the human condition by claiming that it has always existed. The portions on the Middle Ages simply describes some examples of rape from literature (the *Niebelungenlied*) and history (Edward III's rape of the Countess of Salisbury). The argument is superficial and flawed at inception by a casual definition of rape that equates human action with animal instincts.

510. Tannahill, Reay. *Sex in History*. New York: Stein and Day, 1982.

Surveys the history of sexual practices and attitudes from prehistoric times to the twentieth century. Focuses primarily on Europe, but does include chapters on China, India, Islam, and it contains two chapters on medieval Europe. Any work that covers so much must necessarily be superficial, but in spite of that, this book is accurate and provides a broad perspective that can be helpful. There is a full bibliography.

511. Taylor, G. Rattray. *Sex in History*. New York: Vanguard Press, 1954.

Attempts to explain the history of sexuality from a Freudian model.

512. Thiolier-Mejean, Suzanne. *Les Poésies Satiriques et Morales des Troubadours du XIIe Siècle à la Fin du XIIIe Siècle*. Paris: A. G. Nizet, 1978.

Analyzes troubadour poetry, considering such themes as worldly decadence, views of women, venal love and one of its results, bastards. This work is both a fine introduction to the world of the poets, and a good reference work for continuing consultation.

513. Toner, B. *The Facts of Rape*. London: Arrow Books, 1977.

Offers a general treatment of rape which includes a chapter on the history of rape law. This chapter begins with a brief look at ancient societies (i.e., Babylonia), but mainly focuses on British law from the medieval centuries through the nineteenth century. Altogether too general, but does include a detailed account of a thirteenth-century rape trial.

514. Tubach, Frederick C. *Index Exemplorum: A Handbook of Medieval Religious Tales*. Helsinki: Suomalainen Tiedeakatemia, 1969.

Presents an index of the 5,400 exempla found in thirty-seven central collections available in modern print. An extremely good guide to references to sexuality in the sources. For example, one may consult the index for tales dealing with rape or incest.

515. Turner, Ernest Sackville. *A History of Courting*. London: Michael Joseph, 1954.

Presents a general and superficial account of courting customs from "cave man" to the twentieth century. The two chapters on the Middle Ages discuss attitudes toward sexuality and argue that the early church tolerated marriage but did not permit courtship, so the art was lost until the twelfth-century troubadours.

516. Usener, Hermann. *Legenden der Heiligen Pelagia*. Bonn: A. Marcus, 1879.

Argues that the transvestite saint stories were remnants of the cult of the bisexual Aphroditos of Cyprus, to whom women sacrificed in men's clothing and vice versa. This old work has been largely discredited and replaced by newer theories.

517. Ussel, Jozef Maria Willem. *Histoire de la Répression Sexuelle*. Paris: R. Laffont, 1972.

518. Van Hoecke, W., *et al.*, eds. *Love and Marriage in the Twelfth Century*. Leuven: Leuven University Press, 1981.

Collects French and German papers on love and marriage in the twelfth century.

519. Vangaard, Thorkil. *Phallos: A Symbol and its History in the Male World*. New York: International University Press, Inc., 1972.

Examines phallic worship from prehistoric Scandinavians, to Greeks and Romans, early Christians, Medieval Scandinavians, heretics, and witches, with digressions to baboons and anal eroticism. It is a particularly important work, since too many studies of sexuality consider primarily female sexuality giving little note to phallic eroticism.

520. Veith, Ilza. *Hysteria: The History of a Disease.* Chicago: University of Chicago Press, 1965.

Purports to examine the history of hysteria, which from the classical world had been associated with sexuality. Sees the Middle Ages as dominated by the idea of illness in general and hysteria in particular as caused by demons (an idea the author attributes to Augustine), and thus includes discussions of early modern witch hunts in the section on the Middle Ages as being quintessentially medieval. The whole analysis of the Middle Ages is flawed by generalizations that more sophisticated studies have refuted.

521. Veyne, Paul, ed. *A History of Private Life: I. From Pagan Rome to Byzantium.* Translated by Arthur Goldhammer. Cambridge, MA: Harvard University Press, 1987.

Contains a long section on the early Middle Ages in the West, which includes a discussion of attitudes of sexuality written with sensitivity and the solid attention to theory that is a hallmark of the *Annales* school of history. The narrative is continued in volume two, edited by Georges Duby (item 366).

522. Veze, Raoul [Hervez, Jean]. *Ruffians et Ribaudes au Moyen Age.* Paris: Bibliothèque des Curieux, 1913.

Studies primarily the history of prostitution in medieval France, including regulations of prostitution, its regulation by the *rex ribaldorum* at the royal court, and general descriptions of prostitution in Paris and the provinces. The discussion ranges further than prostitution, however, mentioning homosexuality, bestiality, incest, sodomy, and transvestite saints. Not a scholarly work.

523. *Vie Privée et ordre public à la fin du moyen-âge: Etudes sur Manosque, la Provence et le Piémont (1250-1450)*. Aix-en-Provence: Université de Provence, 1987.

Collects a number of articles on the general subject of the interaction between private and public life. Includes topics on sexuality and morality.

524. Watkins, Oscar Daniel. *A History of Penance, Being a Study of the Authorities*. London: Longmans, Green & Co., 1920.

Traces the history of penance from the Apostolic period through the Fourth Lateran Council of 1215. Offers a detailed, careful study that reveals the development of penance for sexual sins (fornication, adultery, etc.).

525. Witte, Heinrich. *Der letzte Puller von Hohenburg*. Strassburg: Heitz & Mundel, 1893.

Studies the life story of the homosexual knight Richard von Hohenburg to illustrate the social and judicial practices of dealing with male homosexuality in fifteenth-century Germany. By this time, homosexuality was equated with heresy, so although Richard fled to Zurich, he was finally executed for his sexual orientation.

526. Ziolkowski, Jan. *Alan of Lille's Grammar of Sex*. Cambridge, MA: Medieval Academy of America, 1985.

Investigates thoroughly Alan of Lille's grammatical metaphors. While Ziolkowski focuses more on the place of grammar in medieval thought in general than on any social framework of sexuality, this work is critical for an understanding of Alan's work, *The Plaint of Nature* (item 179), and the sexual metaphors that are the underpinnings for his attack on homosexuality.

SECONDARY SOURCES

ARTICLES

527. Acquaviva, Sabina. "Costume sessuale e cambiamento sociale in una società in transizione: il caso italiano." *Concilium* 20/3 (1984): 49-60.

528. Aiken, Pauline. "The Summoner's Malady." *Studies in Philology* 33 (1936): 40-44.

Disagrees with Curry (item 353) who claimed the Summoner suffered from leprosy. Maintains instead that the Summoner had scabies, and that the cure involved abstinence from sexual intercourse, impossible for the "lecherous" Summoner.

529. Albertario, Emilio. "Honor matrimonii e affectio maritalis." *Studi di Diritto Romano* 1 (1933): 195-210.

530. Alford, John A. "The Grammatical Metaphor: A Survey of its Use in the Middle Ages." *Speculum* 57,4 (October 1982): 728-60.

Includes examples of the frequent use of sexual references within a larger discussion of the general use of grammatical metaphors, particularly in poetry and in Alan of Lille's *De Planctu Naturae*. Points to the importance of puns and metaphors within the sources.

531. Amundson, D.W., *et al.* "The Age of Menarche in Medieval Europe." *Human Biology* 43 (1973): 363-68.

Reviews medical sources from the sixth through the fifteenth centuries for references to the onset of menstruation. Discovered that the age of menarche commonly ranged from twelve to fifteen.

532. Andreer, M. "Divorce et adultère dans le droit romain classique." *Revue Historique de droit français et étranger* 4e ser. 35 (1957): 1-32.

Summarizes the development of law on adultery and divorce in the late Roman period. Also furnishes a good background for understanding medieval developments in canon law.

533. Anonymous. "Spuren von Kontrarsexualität bei den alten Skandinaviern." *Jahrbuch fur sexuelle Zwischenstufen* 4 (1902): 244-63.

534. Anson, John. "The Female Transvestite in Early Monasticism." *Viator* 5 (1974): 1-32.

Discusses the hagiographic theme of women dressing as men and argues that it was preserved in monasteries by monks attempting to overcome their fears of women and of sexual temptation.

535. Antonucci, Giovanni. "Temi Fallici Nell'Iconografia Medievale." *Il Folklore Italiano* 8 (1933): 61-67.

Argues that phallic worship in the Middle Ages was effective in warding off the evil eye.

536. Ariés, Philippe. "Prostitution, Jeunesse et société dans les villes du Sud-est." *Annales ESC* (1976): 289-325.

537. ——. "Fraternités de jeunesse et niveau de culture dans les villes du Sud-est...." *Cahiers d'histoire* (1976): 67-102.

538. Aróstegui, Antonio. "El Control de Natalidad Según San Agustín." *Religión y Cultura* 11 (1966): 95-106.

Analyzes Augustine's views of the purposes of sexual intercourse within marriage to show that Augustine recognized different times required different actions. Argues, therefore, that Augustine would not disapprove of contraception in these times when overpopulation is a problem.

539. Askew, Melvin W. "Courtly Love: Neurosis as Institution." *Psychoanalytic Review* 52 (1965): 19-29.

Argues the whole tradition of courtly love is a neurotic reaction to clerical teaching of sex as sin, writing "Now if there is one word which characterizes the entire council of courtly lovers,...that word is sick." This is neither a profound nor convincing argument.

540. Astolfi, Riccardo. "Femina probosa, concubina, mater solitaria." *Studia et Documenta Historia et Iuris* 31 (1965): 15-60.

541. Bandini, Vicenzo. "Appunti in tema de reato di adulterio." *Studi in memoria di Umberto Ratti*. Milan: A. Giuffre, 1934, pp. 497-507.

Considers the legal development of adultery treated as a criminal offense from ancient Roman law to medieval jurists, and analyzes the contradictions within the sources.

542. Bapst, Germain. "L'Orfèvrerie d'étain dans l'antiquité." *Revue Archéologique,* Third Series vol 3: 99-100.

Describes phallic designs carried by medieval pilgrims.

543. Barni, Gian Luigi. "Un contrato di concubinato in Corsica nel XIII secolo." *Rivista di storici del diritto italiano* 22 (1949): 131-55.

544. Bassan, Maurice. "Chaucer's 'Cursed Monk', Constantinus Africanus." *Medieval Studies* XXIV (1962): 127-40.

Studies Constantine Africanus, author of the medical tract, "De Coitu," and considers Chaucer's contradictory references to him. Includes a summary of the contents of the text, "De Coitu." See Paul Delany's translation of the text, item 257. For further development of Bassan's argument, see Delany, item 602.

545. Baum, Paul F. "Chaucer's Puns." *Publication of the Modern Language Association* 71 (1956): 225-46.

Lists the puns found in Chaucer, including some that have sexual meanings.

546. Baylan, Michael. "The Galenic and Hippocratic Challenges to Aristotle's Conception Theory." *Journal of the History of Biology* 17, no. 1 (Spring 1984): 83-112.

Summarizes the differences and similarities between the Galenic two-seed theory of reproduction and Aristotle's single-seed theory and discusses the part played by female orgasm in both theories. Provides background for medieval work.

547. Bayle, Gustave. "Notes pour l'Histoire de la Prostitution au Moyen âge dan le Provinces Méridionales de la France." *Mémoires de l'Académie de Vaucluse* 6 (1887): 233-45.

548. Benton, John F. "Clio and Venus: An Historical View of Medieval Love." *The Meaning of Courtly Love.* Edited by F.X. Newman. Albany, NY: State University of New York Press, 1969, pp. 19-42.

Proposes to reconsider the literary concept of courtly love by adding an historical dimension to the discussion. Includes questions of adultery and sexual desire.

549. Bettica-Giovannini, Renato. "Igiene dell'atto sessuale negli aforismi del 'Regimen Sanitatis' del Scuola Salernitana." *Rassegna di Clinica* 57 (1958): 88-92.

550. Biller, P.P.A. "Birth-Control in the West in the 13th and early 14th centuries." *Past and Present* 94 (1982): 3-26.

Seeks to break away from previous historiography which argues for a minimal medieval use of contraception (a full historiographic discussion is included in the article), and introduces the possibility that by the 14th century birth control was widely used. A convincing beginning that calls for further study.

551. Blanchard, Raphael. "Persistance du Culte Phallique en France." *Bulletin de la Société Française d'Histoire de la Médecine,* vol. III (1904): 106-21.

Describes medieval amulets containing phallic symbols.

552. Bloch, Howard. "The Fabliaux, Fetishism and Freud's Jewish Jokes." *Representations* 4 (1983): 1-26.

Attempts to explain the fabliaux in terms of Freudian analysis -- "the fabliaux seem 'to speak' and 'to make speak' questions central to Freudian and post-Freudian analysis." The author sees Freud's analysis of jokes and fetishism as central to an understanding of the tales. The article is intriguing, but more analysis is needed to make the validity of the approach convincing.

553. Bloch, Iwan. "Die Homosexualität in Koln am Ende des 15. Jahrhunderts." *Jahrbuch für Sexualwissenschaft* 1 (1908): 528-35.

554. Bond, Gerald. "*Iocus Amoris:* The Poetry of Baudri of Bougueil and the Formation of the Ovidian Subculture." *Traditio* 42 (1986): 143-92.

Summarizes the life and analyzes some of the poems of a neglected, but influential late eleventh-century abbot. Shows how he favored themes of playful love. Some erotic poetry is addressed to young boys, and Bond discusses the possible homosexual meaning within even friendship poems. This is a comprehensive and scholarly article.

555. Boswell, John. "Towards the Long View: Revolutions, Universals and Sexual Categories." *Salmagundi* 56 (1982/83): 89-113.

Presents a thought-provoking essay on homosexuality, how it is perceived by societies and how it is studied by historians. Uses some medieval examples, but this article will be best used for medievalists for methodological considerations.

556. Bowden, Betsy. "The Art of Courtly Copulation." *Medievalia et Humanistica* 9 (1979): 67-85.

Analyzes perceptively the sexual puns in Andreas Capellanus' "De Amore," which have not been adequately translated in English versions of the work. Bowden suggests the nature of such puns might support psychoanalytic interpretations of Andreas himself. While the argument of historic psychoanalytic neurosis is not convincing, Bowden's analysis of the language itself is excellent. Compare with a similar analysis of the language by Bruno Roy, item 764.

557. Brown, Emerson Jr. "Epicurus and voluptas in Late antiquity: The Curious Testimony of Martianus Capella." *Traditio* 38 (1982): 75-106.

Studies Martianus' "De Nuptiis Philologiae et Mercurii" to explore his treatment of Epicurus. Also considers his treatment of sexuality and discovers that Martianus reveals an approval of sexual pleasure buried in this difficult and confusing tract.

558. ——. "*Hortus Inconclusus:* The Significance of Priapus and Pyramus and Thisbe in the *Merchant's Tale.*" *Chaucer Review* 4 (1969/70): 31-40.

Argues that Chaucer's medieval audience would have understood Priapus to represent both an erotic phallic deity and a comic lecherous figure.

559. ——. "Priapus and the *Parlement of Foulys.*" *Studies in Philology* 72 (1975): 258-74.

Argues that in the *Parlement of Foulys*, Chaucer provides a balanced view of sexuality, neither "to eradicate sensual passion,...nor to deify it."

560. Brown, Peter R.L. "Sexuality and Society in the Fifth Century A.D.: Augustine and Julian of Eclanum." *Tria Cordi. Scritti in onore di Arnaldo Momigliano.* Edited by E. Gabba. Como: Biblioteca di Athenaeum, 1983, pp. 49-70.

Describes the attitudes towards sexuality expressed in the dialogue between Augustine and Julian of Eclanum. For a fuller treatment, See Brown, item 321.

561. Brownlee, Marina S. "Language and Incest in *Grisel y Mirabella*." *Romanic Review* 79,1 (January 1988): 107-28.

Analyzes the relationship between language, incest and tragedy in the fifteenth-century Spanish work by Juan de Flores as well as in Boccaccio's (item 98) early version of one of his tales (Day IV,1). Considers incest, homosexuality and the naturalness of desire.

562. Brucker, Gene A. "The Florentine *Popolo Minuto* and its Political Role, 1340-1450." *Violence and Civil Disorder in Italian Cities 1200-1500* (item 444), pp. 155-83.

Includes a description of prostitution in Florence.

563. Brundage, James A. "'Allas! That Evere Love Was Synne': Sex and Medieval Canon Law." *Catholic Historical Review* 72 (1986): 1-13.

Outlines the development of sex regulation in canon law. Dealt with more fully in Brundage, item 323.

564. ——. "Carnal Delight: Canonistic Theories of Sexuality." *Proceedings of the 5th International Congress of Medieval Canon Law*. Edited by S. Kuttner. Vatican City: Biblioteca Apostolica Vaticana, 1980, pp. 361-85.

Summarizes attitudes about sexuality in canonists from Gratian to the eve of the Council of Trent. Includes an analysis of the canonist views on the sexuality of women; why they saw women as primarily sexual when Romans (and their law) had attributed sexual desires more to males.

565. ——. "The Crusader's Wife: A Canonist Quandary." *Studia Gratiana* 12 (1967): 425-41.

Depicts canonists wrestling with the question of the conflicting vows between a crusader's marital obligation (which would presumably save his wife from falling into infidelity) and the vow to go on crusade. Written with Professor Brundage's usual impressive command of the canonist sources.

566. ——. "Let Me Count the Ways." *Journal of Medieval History* 10 (1984): 81-93.

Examines canonists' and theologians' views on "coital positions." Scholarly and riveting.

567. ——. "Marriage and Sexuality in the Decretals of Pope Alexander III." *Miscellanea Rolando Bandinelli Papa Allessandro III*. Edited by Filippo Liotta. Siena: Accademia senese degli intronati, 1986, pp 59-83.

Outlines material dealt with more fully in Brundage, item 323.

568. ——. "Matrimonial Politics in Thirteenth-Century Aragon: Moncada c. Urgel." *Journal of Ecclesiastical History* 31 (1980): 271-82.

Recounts a good story of a disputed Aragonese marriage, within which emerges testimony about impotence, fornication and "unnatural intercourse."

569. ——. "Prostitution in the Medieval Canon Law." *Signs* 1 (1976): 825-45.

Summarizes perceptions of prostitution from the point of view of the canon lawyers. Includes discussions of male and female sexuality, prevalence of prostitution and possibilities for the prostitute to reform. Additionally, it is extremely valuable for the notes to guide one to the canonist sources.

570. ——. "Rape and Marriage in Medieval Canon Law." *Revue de Droit Canonique* 62 (1978): 62-75.

Investigates the role canon lawyers played in defining "rape," which shaped our modern ideas of the term. Begins with Roman law and Germanic law, but focuses on Gratian's role in adding unlawful intercourse to the abduction of a woman as part of the definition. This article also discusses the establishment of a hierarchy of sex crimes, i.e., seduction, adultery and rape.

571. ——. "Sumptuary Laws and Prostitution in Late Medieval Italy." *Journal of Medieval History* 13 (1987): 343-55.

Points out that sumptuary laws began to be passed in the middle of the thirteenth century, and regulated the clothing of prostitutes as well as that of other women.

572. Bullough, Vern L. "Female Longevity and Diet in the Middle Ages." *Speculum* 55 (1980): 317-25.

Maintains that women had a longer life expectancy in the later Middle Ages because everyone ate more meat and beans. This helped everyone live longer, but especially women who needed more iron due to menstruation and childbirth.

573. ——. "Heresy, Witchcraft and Sexuality." *Journal of Homosexuality* 1,2 (1976): 183-201.

Shows that in the late Middle Ages, sexual diversity became linked with witchcraft and heresy. Discusses charges of sexual license against Albigensians, Waldensians, male transvestites, witches and the Knights Templars, and argues most such charges were false.

574. ——. "Medieval Medical and Scientific Views of Women." *Viator* 4 (1973): 485-501.

Argues that medieval misogyny did not derive solely from religious writers, but that ancient medical and scientific writings also contributed to the belief in female inferiority.

575. ——. "The Prostitute in the Middle Ages." *Studies in Medieval Culture* 10 (1976): 9-18.

Considers the differing approaches to prostitutes by Roman and Medieval cultures. Romans considered prostitutes low status outcasts, but the medieval tradition saw a prostitute as "a weak and strayed person who could be saved."

576. ——. "Sex Education in Medieval Christianity." *Journal of Sex Research* 13 (1977): 185-96.

Argues that sex education (that is, the inculcation of the attitude that sex was sinful) was accomplished in two ways: negatively, through penitentials and confession, and positively, through examples of transvestite saints and reformed prostitutes.

577. ——. "Transvestites in the Middle Ages." *Journal of Sociology* 79 (1974): 1381-94.

Argues the main motive for cross-dressing was to enhance status, therefore women did it without too much disapproval, since their status was improved. Men's cross-dressing was not accepted because it involved a loss of status.

578. Burke, James F. "Juan Ruiz, the Serranas, and the Rites of Spring." *Journal of Medieval and Renaissance Studies* 5 (1975): 13-35.

Maintains that the episode in the center of the *Book of Good Love* expresses a Carnival tradition of spring sexuality and renewal. Draws from Spanish folklore to build his argument.

579. Cadden, Joan. "It Takes All Kinds: Sexuality and Gender Differences in Hildegard of Bingen's 'Book of Compound Medicine'." *Traditio* 40 (1984): 149-71.

Explains Hildegard of Bingen's medical tract, and treats fully and clearly the sexual characteristics and reproductive contributions of women and men.

580. ——. "Medieval Scientific and Medical Views of Sexuality: Questions of Propriety." *Medievalia et Humanistica,* n.s. 14 (1986): 157-71.

Argues that Christian ethics did not prevent medieval medical and scientific writings from including explicit discussions of sexuality and reproduction (including information about contraception and abortion).

581. Callewaert, R.S. "Les pénitentiels du moyen âge et les pratiques anticonceptionnelles." *Supplément de la vie spirituelle* 18 (1965): 339-66.

582. Cantarella, Eva. "Adulterio, omicidio legittimo e causa d'onore in diritto romano." *Studi in onore di Gaetano Scherillo,* vol. 1. Milan: 1972, pp. 243-74.

Provides the background for understanding canon law on the issue of legitimate homicide for adultery by tracing the Roman antecedents in the lex Julia and includes a discussion of the influence of Greek law on the subject.

583. Castelli, Guglielmo. "Il concubinato e la legislazione Augustea." *Bullettino dell'Istituto de Diritto Romano* 27 (1914): 55-71.

584. Chalande, M.J. "La Maison Publique Municipale aux XVe et XVIe siècles a Toulouse." *Mémoires de l'Académie des Sciences, Inscriptions et Belles Lettres de Toulouse,* 10th ser. II (1911): 65-86.

Studies the institution of the brothel in Toulouse.

585. Church, F. Forrester. "Sex and Salvation in Tertullian." *Harvard Theological Review* (April 1975): 83-101.

Defends Tertullian against attribution of sexism for his position on women and sexuality.

586. Clark, Elizabeth A. "Vitiated Seeds and Holy Vessels: Augustine's Manichaean Past." *Ascetic Piety and Women's Faith.* Edited by Elizabeth A. Clark. Lewiston: Edwin Mellen Press, 1986, pp. 291-352.

Explains Augustine's understanding of the relationship between original sin and the scientific facts of the transfer of sperm during intercourse. An important work for understanding Augustine's views on sex that have been so influential in the West.

587. Clifford, John J. "The Ethics of Conjugal Intimacy according to St. Albert the Great." *Theological Studies* 3 (1942): 10-26.

Reviews and analyzes Albert's views in *Debitum Marital*. Albert argues 1) that coitus in marriage is not inherently sinful, 2) concupiscence needs forgiveness, and 3) the antidote to concupiscence is found in marriage.

588. Coleman, Janet. "The Owl and the Nightingale and Papal Theories of Marriage." *Journal of Ecclesiastical History* 38,4 (October, 1987): 517-68.

Argues that the late twelfth-century poem, *Owl and the Nightingale*, is a debate poem that mirrors developing canon law positions on marriage. Within the debate, the two birds articulate views of adultery, lust, and marital and extra-marital relations. Includes the text and translation of the poem.

589. Coleman, John. "La rivoluzione omosessuale e l'ermeneutica." *Concilium* 20/3 (1984): 208-24.

590. Cooper, Kate Mason. "Elle and L: Sexualized Textuality in *Le Roman de Silence*." *Romance Notes* 25,3 (Spring 1985): 341-60.

Studies the thirteenth-century French romance in which a woman lives as a man and uses language to analyze portrayals of male and female sexuality.

591. Coupe, M.D. "The Personality of Guibert de Nogent Reconsidered." *Journal of Medieval History* 9 (1983): 317-29.

Disputes Kantor's (item 666) psycho-historical assessment of Guibert and argues that the monk was not shaped by an unresolved oedipal complex nor a fear of castration. Psycho-historical analyses are easy to attack, and this article provides little special insights other than the dispute.

592. Courouve, Claude. "Sodomy Trials in France." *Gay Books Bulletin* 1 (1979): 22-23,26.

Lists fifty-three sodomy trials involving sixty-six accused between 1317 and 1783. Argues that capital punishment for sodomy was only enforced after the medieval period.

593. Covi, Davide. "L'etica sessuale paradisiaca agostiniana." *Laur* 3 (1972): 340-64.

594. ———. "El Fin de la Actividad Sexual Según San Agustín." *Augustinus* 17/65-68 (1972): 47-65.

Analyzes the thought of Saint Augustine on the purpose of sexual intercourse, noting that for the Bishop, sexual activity has its place in the natural and social order, notably for procreation. Any activity which is "unnatural" (including prostitution and practicing anal sex) is wrong. Covi further considers whether abstaining from intercourse altogether would be legitimate in the Augustinian system.

595. ———. "Il valore ontologico della sessualità umana secondo S. Agostino." *Laur* 2 (1970): 375-95.

596. Crompton, Louis. "The Myth of Lesbian Impunity: Capital Laws from 1270 to 1791." *Journal of Homosexuality* 6 (1980/81): 1-25.

Disputes the claim that lesbian acts were ignored in medieval law. Identifies an early secular law against lesbianism in 1270. The early documentation articulates the existence of lesbianism, but the author fails to demonstrate much actual persecution of lesbians before the Renaissance, although the evidence for after that time is convincing.

597. Deanesly, M., *et al.* "The Canterbury edition of the answers of Pope Gregory I to St. Augustine." *Journal of Ecclesiastical History* 10 (1959): 1-49.

Maintains that the answers of Gregory I that are reproduced in Bede's *Historia Ecclesiastica* are authentically Gregorian, but were written separately, not as one tract. This document is particularly important, since it has traditionally been used to articulate Gregory I's views on sex.

598. Dedek, John F. "Premarital Sex: The Theological Argument from Peter Lombard to Durand." *Theological Studies* 41 (1980): 643-67.

Surveys twelfth through early fourteenth-century theologians' views on fornication. Concludes that they prohibited fornication not because it was intrinsically evil, but because it was prohibited by natural law of the common good. The author is asking the question, "Is fornication bad because it is forbidden, or is it forbidden because it is bad?" This article is for those interested in fine legal distinctions.

599. ———. "Moral Absolutes in the Predecessors of St. Thomas." *Theological Studies* 38 (1977): 654-80.

Presents a legalistic analysis of the theologians who preceded Thomas to explain to what degree they believed in moral absolutes. Includes considerations of fornication and incest.

600. ———. "Intrinsically Evil Acts: An Historical Study of the Mind of St. Thomas." *Thomist* 43 (1979): 385-413.

Offers an erudite study of St. Thomas and his intellectual tradition to consider whether he believed any acts were "intrinsically evil." This article is for the specialist, or those with some background in scholasticism. Not for the casual reader.

601. Delahaye, Philippe. "Development of the Medieval Church's Teaching on Marriage." *The Future of Marriage as Institution: Concilium 55.* Edited by Franz Böekle. New York: Herder & Herder, 1970, pp. 83-88.

Brief and undocumented discussion of marriage, including a consideration of whether consent or consummation validated a marriage.

602. Delany, Paul. "Constantinus Africanus and Chaucer's *Merchant's Tale.*" *Philological Quarterly* 46 (1967): 560-66.

Build's upon Bassan's article (item 544) and looks more closely at "the sexual attitudes and prescriptions found within 'De Coitu.'" Further compares Constantinus' text with January's actions in the *Merchant's Tale* to add to our understanding of Chaucer's intentions.

603. De La Taille, M. "Le Péché Véniel dans la Théologie de S. Thomas d'après un Livre Récent." *Gregorianum* 7 (1926): 28-43.

604. Deman, T. "Le Péché de Sensualité." *Melanges Mandonnet* I (1930): 265-83.

Reviews the origins of Thomas Aquinas' thought on the sin of sensuality, in which the "sensual appetite" takes over. Clearly explains Thomas' thought and places it in the context of other medieval thinkers, showing the antecedents of Thomas' work.

605. Denomy, Alexander J. "The *De Amore* of Andreas Capellanus and the Condemnation of 1277." *Medieval Studies* 8 (1946): 107-49.

Studies Andreas' *De Amore* and explains the ideas of sexuality and love in the text that caused it to be condemned by the Bishop of Paris in 1277. Provides an excellent explication of Andreas' thought.

606. ——. "Fin Amors." *Medieval Studies*, 7 (1945): 139-207.

Argues against the idea that there were two kinds of love praised in the troubadour tradition: idealized and real. Claims instead that there was only one kind, sensual, carnal and incorporating everything that generates desire (touching, kissing, nudity, etc.), but stops short of intercourse. He calls it a "love of desire divorced entirely from physical possession." Further maintains that the concept comes from the Moslems, and he looks to Avicenna for similar ideas.

607. Derouet-Besson, Marie-Claude. "Inter duos scopulos: Hypothèses sur la place de la sexualité dans modèles de...xie siècle." *Annales, ESC* 36 (1981): 922-45.

Examines the place of sexuality in the world-views of the 11th century. Three different views are described: 1) heretical view, a dualist view that denigrated sex: 2) monastic view, influential view that also denigrated sex, and 3) resistance to this negation - those who fought clerical celibacy requirements and said sex in marriage was good.

608. De Waha, Michel. "Note sur l'usage de moyen contraceptifs à Bruxelles au debut du XVe Siècle." *Annales de la Société Belge d'Histoire des Hôpitaux* 13 (1975): 3-28.

609. Donaldson, E. Talbot. "Medieval Poetry and Medieval Sin." *Speaking of Chaucer*. New York: Norton, 1970, pp. 164-75.

Offers an easy-to-read brief discussion on what kind of marital intercourse would constitute venial or mortal sin in England during the time of Chaucer.

610. Dubarle, A.M. "La Bible et les Pères ont-ils parlé de la contraception?" *Supplement de la Vie Spirituelle* 15 (1962): 373-610.

611. ——. "La Contraception chez Césaire d'Arles." *Supplement de la Vie Spirituelle* 16 (1963): 515-19.

612. Dufresne, Jean-Luc "Les comportements amoureux d'après le registre de l'officialité de Cerisy." *Bulletin philologique et historique (jusqu'à 1610) du Comité des travaux historiques et scientifique* (1973): 131-56.

Studies late fourteenth and fifteenth-century records of parish visits to consider three categories of faults: 1) marriage irregularities, 2) concubinage, 3) prostitution and general debauchery. Explores an excellent source to get at hard-to-reach practices and attitudes about sex.

613. Elsasser, G. "Ausfall des Coitus als Krankheitsursache in der Medizin des Mittelalters." *Abhandlungen zur Geschichte der*

Medizin und der Naturwissenschaften 3 (1934): 15-20.

614. Engbring, G.M. "Saint Hildegard, Twelfth-Century Physician." *Bulletin of the History of Medicine* 8 (1940): 770-84.

Intends only to be an introduction to Hildegard's medical writings (including those on sexuality). For a more complete discussion, see Cadden, item 579.

615. Fenster, Thelma. "Beaumanoir's *La Manekine:* Kin D(r)ead: Incest, Doubling, and Death." *American Imago: A Psychoanalytic Journal for Culture, Science, and the Arts* 39,1 (1982): 41-58.

Argues that the French Romance, *La Manekine* (which begins with incestuous desire between father and daughter) may be interpreted at a psychoanalytic level of Oedipal complex and castration fear.

616. Ferckel, Christoph. "Die Secreta Mulierum und ihr Verfasser." *Sudhoffs Archiv für Geschichte der Medizin und der Naturwissenschaften* 38 (1954): 267-74.

Studies the pseudo-Albertan medical tract and argues that it differs from Albert's other works. See item 245, for the text, and Lynn Thorndike, item 795, for a counter-argument.

617. Fisher, John H. "Tristan and Courtly Adultery." *Comparative Literature* 9 (1957): 150-64.

Argues that the origin of the "cult" of adultery in *Tristan* and *Lancelot* looked back to Pictish matrilineal society that did not preclude polyandry (i.e., Iseut could have lived happily with both Mark and Tristan). The author sees in the tension in the twelfth-century romances an echo of an old struggle between patriarchal Celts who replaced matrilineal Picts. This thesis raises more questions than it answers.

618. Flandrin, Jean Louis. "Contraception, mariage et relations amoureuses dans l'Occident Chrétien." *Annales ESC* 24 (1969): 1370-90.

Reviews legislation and other texts against contraception in the Middle Ages to the eighteenth century, and looks at changes in attitude over time as change occurred in perceptions of marriage. Excellent article with valuable notes.

619. ——. "Mariage tardif et vie sexuelle: discussions et hypothèses de recherche." *Annales, ESC* 27 (1972): 1351-78.

Reviews masturbation and the development of prohibitions against it. Contains a good discussion of Gerson's fourteenth-century comments, although most of the article is post-medieval.

620. ——. "Repression and Change in the Sexual Life of Young People in Medieval and Early Modern Times." *Journal of Family History* 2 (1977): 196-210.

Enters the controversy about whether society had undergone "eroticization" or repression before the twentieth century, and concludes that both phenomena can be observed. He argues that the Middle Ages recognized and accepted youthful sexual urges, expressed in early marriage, prostitution, rape and courtly behavior. Later, this was repressed at the same time society as a whole valued eroticism.

621. Fraser, Douglas. "The Heraldic Woman: A Study in Diffusion." *The Many Faces of Primitive Art, a Critical Anthology*. Edited by Douglas Fraser. New Jersey: Prentice-Hall, 1966, pp. 36-99.

Describes the many instances that a female figure was portrayed with her legs apart displaying her genitals, and includes a discussion of the Romanesque tradition. The analysis seems flawed by his comparison of figures that have considerable differences - i.e., breasts or not, attendants or not. See Jørgen Andersen, item 294, for a fuller treatment of the medieval material.

622. Friedman, Lionel J. "Gradus Amoris." *Romance Philology* 19 (1965): 167-77.

Examines a medieval literary convention that pervaded erotic literature that said there were five steps in the process of love: sight, conversation, touch, kiss and deed. The author demonstrates this convention dated from antiquity, traces its use through the Middle Ages, and shows how it ordered the narrative sequence in *Roman de la Rose*.

623. Gaidoz, Henri. "Le Dieu Gaulois du Soleil et le Symbolisme de la Roue." *Revue Archéologique* (antiquité et moyen âge) Third series vol. V: 370-71.

Describes medieval phallic amulets found in the Seine.

624. Gehl, Paul. "Texts and Textures: Dirty Pictures and other Things in Medieval Manuscripts." *Corona* 3 (1983): 68-77.

Studies a series of sexual and scatological illustrations in a fourteenth-century grammarbook (University of Chicago Ms. 99) written ca. 1390 at Pisa. The author explains the probable punning and other mnemonic associations of the drawings. For a response to this article, see Moore, item 717.

625. Goodich, Michael. "Sodomy in Ecclesiastical Law and Theory." *Journal of Homosexuality*, 1, no. 4. (1976): 427-34.

Provides a remarkably complete survey of legislation on sodomy in a short article. Includes the scholastic theology of Anselm of Laon, Peter Lombard, Thomas Aquinas, William Peraldus, and canon lawyers (particularly Gratian and Gregory IX).

626. ——. "Sodomy in Medieval Secular Law." *Journal of Homosexuality* 1, no. 3. (1976): 295-302.

Examines the thirteenth-century association of sodomy with heresy in secular laws that led to severe penalties for homosexual acts and persecution by the Inquisition. Focuses primarily on Italian evidence.

627. Grabmann, M. "Das Werk *De Amore* des Andreas Capellanus und das Verurteilungsdektret des Bischofs Stephen Tempier von Paris vom 7. März 1277." *Speculum* 7 (1932): 75-79.

Identifies a tract condemned by the Bishop of Paris in 1277 as Andreas' *De Amore,* and explains its condemnation as based on its position on certain sexual matters, such as the definition of "pure" and "mixed" love.

628. Granville, Anna. "Compagnetto da Prato: A Sophisticated Jongleur." *Cultura Neolatina* XIX (1959): 35-45.

Presents and analyzes two love poems, of which one moves rapidly to physical consummation with the aid of magic.

629. Gravdal, Kathryn. "Camouflaging Rape: The Rhetoric of Sexual Violence in the Medieval Pastourelle." *Romanic Review* (1985): 361-73.

Confronts the prevalence of rape in the popular medieval pastourelles (1/5 of the surviving poems portray forced intercourse) and calls modern medievalists to task for not taking this theme seriously. A fine article.

630. Green, Monica. "Women's Medical Practice and Health Care in Medieval Europe." *Signs* 14 (Winter 1989): 434-73.

Challenges the assumptions that in the Middle Ages "women's health was women's business," and reconsiders who actually cared for women (placing special emphasis on gynecological and obstetrical care). Touches on issues of sexuality, but is most useful for its extensive notes pointing to literature on the subject.

631. Greenberg, David. "Christian Intolerance of Homosexuality." *American Journal of Sociology* 88 (1982): 515-48.

Attributes intolerance of homosexuality to two developments: 1)early Christian ascetic movements and 2) Gregorian reforms. Argues against Boswell's (item 310) attribution of repression to decline in urbanization.

632. Grennen, Joseph E. "Chaucer's Monk: Baldness, Venery, and Embonpoint." *American Notes and Queries* 6 (February 1968): 83-85.

Points out the sexual pun that associates venery with coitus, and describes medieval medical citations that yoke baldness and obesity with excessive carnality. Argues that these associations probably shaped Chaucer's description of the monk.

633. Guerra, F. "The Description of Syphilis in Avicenna." *XXVII Congreso Internacional de Historia de la Medicina, Actas.* Barcelona: Academia de Ciencies Mediques de Catalunya i Balears, 1981, pp. 74-96.

Maintains that Avicenna's descriptions prove the existence of syphilis in medieval Europe. Compare this view with that of Grmek, item 394, who argues to the contrary.

634. ———. "The Dispute over Syphilis: Europe versus America." *Clio Medica* 13 (1978), pp. 39-61.

Provides a good summary of the debate.

635. Gutsch, Milton R. "A Twelfth Century Preacher - Fulk of Neuilly." *The Crusades and other Historical Essays presented to Dana C. Munro.* Edited by L.J. Paetow. New York: F.S. Crofts & Co., 1968, pp. 183-206.

Studies a vigorous twelfth-century preacher who attacked the vices, including prostitution, he observed in Paris. The article is brief, but excellent, and will guide the reader to further sources on prostitution.

636. Halverson, John. "Amour and Eros in the Middle Ages." *Psychoanalytic Review* 57 (1970): 245-58.

Disputes successfully the analyses of courtly love proposed by Askew (item 539) and Koenigsberg (item 676). Argues instead that the twelfth century saw "an eruption of eros in Languedoc literature simply because circumstances permitted it," and this expression of love later divided into a "naturalistic" view and a "spiritual" view. The recognition of the historical element as important to the psychology is a welcome addition to this kind of discussion.

637. Harden, A.R. "The Element of Love in the Chansons de Geste." *Annuale Medievale* 5 (1964): 65-80.

Describes women who appear in the *chansons de geste*. Mentions rape in *Floovant,* impotence caused by an herb in *Orson de Beauvais* and other encounters, romantic and sexual. This article merely identifies the occurrences without attempting a synthesis or analysis of the material.

638. Harrington, P.V. "The Impediment of Impotency and the Notion of Male Impotency." *The Jurist* 19 (1959): 29-66.

Contains a full discussion of male potency and what theologians and lawyers from the time of Gratian to the Council of Trent considered that to mean, particularly with regard to the capacity to consummate a marriage.

639. Hawkes, S.C. *et al.* "Crime and Punishment in an Anglo-Saxon Cemetery." *Antiquity* 49 (1975): 118-22.

Reports of an excavation of two skeletons that the authors argue were raped. Their case is compelling, and the article draws from Anglo-Saxon historical works to substantiate the argument.

640. Heinsohn, Gunnar and Otto Steiger. "The Elimination of Medieval Birth Control and the Witch Trials of Modern Times." *International Journal of Women's Studies* 5 (1982): 193-214.

Maintains that during the Middle Ages midwives disseminated information about abortion and birth control, and that the witch trials of the early modern period represented an attempt to eradicate these contraceptive techniques. The argument is developed more fully, but no more convincingly in item 400.

641. Herlihy, David. "Some Psychological and Social Roots of Violence in the Tuscan Cities." *Violence and Civil Disorder in Italian Cities 1200-1500* (item 444), pp. 129-54.

Argues that late medieval Tuscans believed that youthful sex urges contributed most to violence in the cities.

642. Herman, Gerald. "The Sin Against Nature and its Echoes in Medieval French Literature." *Annuale Mediaevale* 17 (1976): 70-87.

Summarizes some of the medieval condemnations of homosexuality, and claims there are comparatively few mentions of homosexuality or sodomy in the vernacular literature of the same period. He further argues that medieval attitudes toward homosexuality were uncompromisingly negative. For a more balanced view, see Boswell, item 310.

643. Herter, Hans. "Die Soziologie der antiken Prostitution im Lichte des heidnischen und christlichen Schrifttums." *Jahrbuch für Antike und Christentum* 3 (1960): 70-110.

Presents a well-documented article dealing with prostitution and rape based primarily on legal sources. Most of the article deals with the classic world, but the author does conclude with the early Middle Ages.

644. Heusler, Andreas. "Die Geschichte vom Völsi, eine altnordische Bekehrungsanekdote." *Zeitschrift des Vereins für Volkskunde*, xiii (1903): 29-35.

Describes phallic worship among the Volsi.

645. Hill, Thomas D. "Narcissus, Pygmalion, and the castration of Saturn: Two Mythographical Themes in the *Roman de la Rose*." *Studies in Philology* 71 (1974): 404-26.

Argues that the lover in the *Roman*, like Pygmalion, is irrational (and highly carnal), yet achieves what Reason defined as the rational end of sexual consummation, impregnating a woman. Further argues that the story of the castration of Saturn reflects an Augustinian view of sexuality that saw a permanent split between reason and sex after the Fall.

646. Hoffman, Marian H. "As the Poet Saw Her: Images of Women in the Pastorals and the Fabliaux." *Proceedings of the 8th Annual Meeting of the Western Society for French History*. Edited by E.L. Newman. Las Cruces, NM: Western Society for French History, 1981, pp. 33-41.

Offers a brief discussion of treatment of women in the fabliaux and pastorals. Shows the frequency of rape as a theme in the pastorals, and considers the misogyny and portrayal of women as insatiably sexual in the fabliaux. The article is too short to provide more than a cursory treatment of the material, and the thesis that the ill treatment of women in the literature is a function of women achieving a degree of personal sovereignty and success is not supported.

647. Honings, V. "L'aborto nei libri penitenziali Irlandesi." *Apollinaris* (1975): 501-23.

648. Hoops, E.H. "Die Sexologischen Kapitel in 'Canon Medicinae' des Avicenna vergleichen mit der Schrift 'De Coitu' des Maimonides." *Aesthetische Medizin* 16 (1967): 305-08.

649. Horowitz, Maryanne Cline. "Aristotle and Women." *Journal of the History of Biology* 9,2 (1976): 183-213.

Analyzes Aristotle's views on women that were influential on the medical views of sexuality during the Middle Ages. Describes Aristotle's view of woman as a "mutilated male" sexually, and includes his embryological analysis. The article takes a feminist view and claims to bring Aristotle's antifeminism to the fore so it may be confronted and counteracted.

650. Howarth, W.D. "'Droit du Seigneur': Fact or Fantasy" *Journal of European Studies* 1 (1971): 291-312.

Surveys thoroughly the historical and anthropological literature on the "Droit du Seigneur," the right of a lord to his vassals' brides' maidenheads. The author argues that this practice never existed, and that we may perhaps, finally, put the fantasy to rest.

651. Humbert, Alphonse. "Les péchés de la sexualité dans le Nouveau Testament." *Studia Moralia* 8 (1970): 149-83.

Catalogues the sexual sins mentioned in the New Testament (including adultery, prostitution, sodomy) and analyzes the meanings of the terms (concentrating on the Greek). Further considers the relative gravity of sexual sins. Provides excellent background for the texts that were so often discussed in the Middle Ages.

652. Huot, Sylvia. "Seduction and Sublimation: Christine de Pizan, Jean de Meun, and Dante." *Romance Notes* 25,3 (Spring 1985): 361-73.

Studies Christine of Pizan's thought on feminism, especially as expressed in the debate on the *Roman de la Rose*. Discusses Christine's criticism of the use of explicit sexual terms and places this critique within a context of Christine's "understanding of the relationship between language and eros."

653. Jackoff, Rachel. "Transgression and Transcendence: Figures of Female Desire in Dante's *Commedia*." *Romanic Review* 79,1 (January 1988): 129-42.

Analyzes three female figures in Dante who were associated with incest, and compares them with the Virgin Mary, a sexually transcendent figure.

654. Jacquart, Danielle and Claude Thomasset. "Albert le Grand et les problèmes de la sexualité." *History and Philosophy of the Life Sciences, Pubblicazioni della Stazione Zoologica di Napoli* 3 (1981): 73-93.

Studies some aspects of Albertus Magnus' views on sexuality and reproduction, notably his position on the controversy over female seed and the relationship between the physical and mental (expressed in masturbation and suitable times for intercourse).

655. ———. "L'Amour 'héroïque' à travers le traité d'Arnaud de Villeneuve." *La Folie et le Corps*. Edited by Jean Ceard. Paris: L'Ecole Normale Supérieure, 1985, pp. 143-58.

Analyzes the relationship between madness and sexuality in the tract of Arnaud of Villeneuve. An analysis that can be helpful in clarifying the text.

656. Jacquart, Danielle. "La Maladie et le Remède d'Amour dans quelques Ecrits Médicaux du Moyen Age." *Acts du Colloque "Amour, Mariage et Transgressions au Moyen Age."* Goppingen: Kümmerle Verlag, 1984, pp. 93-101.

Summarizes medical prescriptions for recovery of obsessive love. An excellent survey.

657. Janssens, L. "Morale Conjugale et Progestogènes." *Ephemerides Theologicae Lovaniensis* 39,4 (1963): 787-826.

Asserts that the outlook of Stoics, Neo-Pythagoreans, Essenes and Gnostics passed a negative view of sexuality into Christianity through St. Augustine.

658. Jeay, Madeleine. "Sexuality and Family in Fifteenth-Century France: Are Literary Sources a Mask or a Mirror?" *Journal of Family History* 4 (1979): 328-45.

Attempts to learn attitudes toward sexuality by looking at rituals and customs governing marriage. Analyzes the *Quinze Joyes de Mariage* to argue the text, although satiric, did mirror societal attitudes, and the prevailing attitude toward sex was "reserve." The argument for "sexual reserve" is not compelling. Other sources (such as the fabliaux) would have to be addressed before one could argue for a repressed society.

659. Jensen, Joseph. "Does Porneia mean Fornication? A Critique of Bruce Malina." *Novum Testamentum* 20 (1978): 161-84.

Disputes Malina, who said porneia does not mean fornication, arguing that the Old Testament did forbid sexual activity between singles and, in any case, the New Testament went beyond Old Testament prohibitions, so porneia does mean fornication. Of course, this should be read in conjunction with Malina's article, item 700.

660. Jernigan, Charles. "The Song of Nail and Uncle: Arnaut Daniel's Sestina 'Lo Ferm Voler q'el Cor m'intra'." *Studies in Philology* 71 (1974): 127-51.

Argues for an interpretation of Arnaut Daniel's sestina that is comic, explicitly sexual, and based on elaborate puns for genitals and intercourse. The argument is well made and convincing. Includes an edition and translation of the poem.

661. Jochens, Jenny. "The Church and Sexuality in Medieval Iceland." *Journal of Medieval History* 24,6 (1980): 377-85.

Creatively analyzes sources to look at the church's attempt to regulate sexual behavior among the newly converted Icelanders. Focuses on clerical celibacy, marriage rules, availability of divorce and prevalence of extramarital sex. Demonstrates that the older, more casual sexual practices were not readily abandoned.

662. Johansson, Warren. "London's Medieval Sodomites." *Cabirion and Gay Books Bulletin* 10 (1984): 5-7,34.

Describes the sexual terminology used in Richard of Devizes' *Chronicle of the Times of King Richard the First* to prove the existence of a homosexual subculture in London in the late 12th century. The evidence does not convincingly prove the thesis, but the article is invaluable to read in conjunction with Richard's Chronicle, particularly since Johansson points out translation errors of sexual terms in Appleby's (item 28) English translation of the source.

663. Jung, Marc-Rene. "Der Rosenroman in der Kritik seit dem 18 Jahrhundert." *Romanische Forschungen* LXXVIII (1966): 203-57.

Compiles a complete annotated bibliography on works on the *Roman de la Rose.*

664. Kalifa, Simon. "Singularités matrimoniales chez les anciens germains." *Revue historique de droit français et étranger 4e ser.* 48 (1970): 199-225.

665. Kanton, Sofía. "Ocho Máscaras para el Requerimiento de Amores: Las 'Serranillas' del Marqués de Santillana." *Boletín de la Real Academía Española* 63 (1983): 393-441.

Presents a structural analysis of fifteenth-century Spanish amorous pastourelles. Argues that these stories are similar in form to comparable twelfth-century stories (that appear, for example, in the *Book of Good Love),* so this analysis illuminates the medieval prototype.

666. Kantor, J. "A Psycho-Historical Source: The Memoirs of Abbot Guibert of Nogent." *Journal of Medieval History* 2 (1976): 281-303.

Offers a psycho-history of Guibert of Nogent, arguing that the monk wrote bad history because he was obsessed with all things sexual, and suffered from castration fears, among other things. Draws heavily from Freudian models, and its usefulness depends upon one's conviction of Freud's applicability to the twelfth century.

667. Karlen, Arno. "The Homosexual Heresy." *Chaucer Review* 6,1 (1971): 44-63.

Summarizes the history of homosexuality in the Middle Ages based largely on dubious secondary sources. Connects homosexuality with a growing urban culture in a cause/effect relationship to explain the "spread of Norman homosexuality to Anglo-Saxon England," and further concludes that people in the Middle Ages associated heresy with sodomy because "the anus is the most despised part of the body."

668. Karras, Ruth Mazo. "The Regulations of Brothels in Later Medieval England." *Signs* 14 (Winter 1989): 399-433.

Discusses brothel regulations in Southwark, England mainly during the late fourteenth and fifteenth centuries, and compares them with similar regulations in other European countries and other towns in England. Includes a translation of the brothel ordinance text in an appendix.

669. Kay, Richard. "The Sin of Brunetto Latini." *Medieval Studies* 31 (1969): 262-86.

Maintains that the sin of Brunetto Latini (described in Dante's *Divine Comedy*) was not sodomy, the sexual sin "against nature," but a "perversion" of the natural order by "forcing philosophy into the service of the unnaturally insubordinate and autonomous Italian Republics," thus a political sin.

670. Kellogg, Robert. "Sex and the Vernacular in Medieval Iceland." *Proceedings of the First International Saga Conference, 1971*. London: Viking Society for Northern Research, 1973, pp. 244-60.

Asserts that the unique situation of Icelandic schools (located at the homes of married priests living on farms with families) led Icelandic intellectuals to be more exposed to normal sexual life than their continental counterparts. However, this article deals more with gender issues and the comfort between men and women rather than sexuality *per se*.

671. Kirby, Steven D. "Juan Ruiz's Serranas: The Archpriest-Pilgrim and Medieval Wild Women." *Hispanic Studies in Honor of Alan D. Deyermond: A North American Tribute*. Madison: Hispanic Seminary of Medieval Studies, 1986, pp. 151-69.

Studies the sexual adventures central to the *Book of Good Love*,and concludes that they emerge from the dual medieval traditions of carnival/pilgrimage and wild women as sexual stereotypes. The article is a thought-provoking introduction to the subject, but not satisfactorily developed.

672. Kirshner, Jane. "Bishops as Marital Advisors in the Ninth Century." *Women of the Medieval World*. Edited by J. Kirshner and Suzanne Wemple. Oxford: Basil Blackwell, 1985, pp. 54-84.

Shows that ninth-century bishops had to advise on marital sex problems such as impotence, and adultery, and weaves these themes into a larger discussion on attitudes toward sex and marriage. A fine article that uses actual cases to good advantage and concludes that churchmen were able to set aside their prejudices toward celibacy and treat wives' sexual problems with compassion.

673. Kismer, Ellen. "The 'noyous humoure of lecherie'." *Art Bulletin*. 57 (1975): 1-8.

Examines the depiction of "luxuria" (lasciviousness and lust for the Middle Ages) in the *Somme le Roi*, a thirteenth-century moral treatise on virtues and vices. The discussion is revealing of perceptions of sexuality, i.e., its associations with beasts and blood.

674. Kittel, Ruth Weisberg. "Rape in Thirteenth-Century England: A Study of the Common-Law Courts." *Women and the Law: A Social Historical Perspective, vol. 2.* Edited by D. Kelly. Cambridge: Cambridge University Press, 1982, pp. 101-15.

Investigates 142 rape cases brought before the justices between 1202 and 1276, and considers why most of the raped women chose not to follow through on the prosecution. A thorough, careful study.

675. Kligerman, Charles. "A Psycho-analytic Study of the Confessions of St. Augustine." *Journal of the American Psychoanalytic Association* 3 (July 1957): 469-84.

Maintains that the *Confessions* is a "psychiatric personal history without the contaminating presence of an interviewer." Further argues that Monica had incestuous desires for Augustine and Augustine suffered from masculine narcissism, and that his life was a struggle between the "City of Rome" of his father, and the "City of God" of his mother. The analysis is as strong as one's commitment to historical psychoanalysis.

676. Koenigsberg, Richard A. "Culture and Unconscious Fantasy: Observations on Courtly Love." *The Psychoanalytic Review* 54 (1967): 36-50.

Asserts that courtly love, particularly as presented by Andreas Capellanus in "De Amore" is "...an institutionalized manifestation of an intense fixation on the mother, its rules being designed to recreate the Oedipal situation." Discusses the themes of incest and masochism implicit within Andreas' work. The article is too ahistoric to be useful for medieval historic or literary analysis. For further psychological interpretations of the phenomenon, see Moller, item 716.

677. Kudlein, F. "The Seven Cells of the Uterus: the Doctrine and its Roots." *Bulletin of the History of Medicine*. 39 (1965): 415-23.

Traces the origins of the medieval medical theory that the uterus contained seven cells, and that boys were conceived if the right cells were impregnated, girls if the left, and hermaphrodites if the center. Demonstrates that this theory was not of medieval origin, but elements of it went back to classical thought.

678. Kusche, Brigitte. "Zur 'Secreta Mulierum' -- Forschung." *Janus* 62 (1975): 103-23.

Summarizes the scholarship on the authorship of the pseudo-Albertan medical tract, "*De Secretis Mulierum*" (item 245).

679. Kuster, H. and R. Kormier. "Old Views and New Trends: Observations on the Problem of Homosexuality in the Middle Ages." *Studi Medievali* 25 (1984): 587-610.

Proposes to update and build upon Boswell's now-classic work on homosexuality (item 310). This article carefully considers the following topics: 1) vocabulary, 2) views on male homosexuality, 3) sexual perversion and sodomy, 4) pro gay sources, 5) female homosexuality, 6) medieval sexuality and procreation, 7) problem of celibate clergy, and 8) psychological aspects. A sound work with excellent bibliographic references.

680. Lacy, G. F. "Augustinian Imagery and Fabliau 'Obscenity'." *Studies on the Seven Sages of Rome...to the Memory of Jean Mesraki*. Edited

by H. Niedzielski. Honolulu: Education Research Association, 1978, pp. 219-30.

Maintains that the authors of the fabliaux, even the obscene ones, drew upon characteristically Augustinian imagery to enhance the humor of the works.

681. Latzke, Therese. "Die Carmina erotica der Ripollsammlung." *Mittellateinisches Jahrbuch* 10 (1975): 138-201.

682. Lavaud, B. "The Interpretation of the Conjugal Act in the Theology of Marriage." *The Thomist* 1 (1939): 360-80.

Analyzes the role and purpose of intercourse in marriage from a theological perspective. Articulates clearly the theological positions for and against the use of birth control. Reproduces clearly many of the arguments used by medieval canonists.

683. Leclercq, Jean. "Modern Psychology and the Interpretation of Medieval Texts." *Speculum* 48 (1973): 476-90.

Brings psychological methods to study a few medieval figures (Othloh of Saint-Emmeran, Stephen of Obazine, Abelard and others) and shows the utility of the method in helping trace motivations. A thoughtful and cautious essay on the subject. While this article does not deal extensively with sexuality, I include it here as a model for using methods of psychology, which are often brought to the study of the history of sexuality.

684. LeGoff, Jacques. "L'Amour et la Sexualité." *L'Histoire* 63 (1984): 52-59.

Summarizes briefly the development of Christian control over sexuality and sexual acts throughout the Middle Ages from the age of the apostles through the Gregorian reform. Translated in item 427.

685. Lemay, Helen Rodnite. "Anthonius Guainerius and Medieval Gynecology." *Women of the Medieval World: Essays in Honor of John H. Mundy*. Edited

by J. Kirshner, and S. Wemple. Oxford: Basil Blackwell, 1985, pp. 317-36.

Reviews the medical work of an early fifteenth-century professor of medicine in Pavia in the course of a general discussion on medieval doctor/patient relationships. The summary includes fifteenth-century opinions on the efficacy of masturbation, intercourse techniques to bring women to orgasm, and the use of midwives.

686. ——. "Some Thirteenth and Fourteenth Century Lectures on Female Sexuality." *International Journal of Women's Studies* 1 (1978): 391-400.

Studies thirteenth- and fourteenth-century lectures based on *On the Secrets of Women* (see item 245). Argues that this tract, along with the commentaries on it, fused the theological views of women with the medical ones saying that women's biological inferiority made them dangerous to men instead of just to themselves. She proves her point convincingly. Included in this article is a discussion of menstruation, wounds to the penis, pregnancy and sterility.

687. ——. "The Stars and Human Sexuality: Some Medieval Scientific Views." *Isis* 71 (1980): 127-37.

Examines Arabic astrology texts that became highly influential in the West in the twelfth and thirteenth centuries. These texts give extensive consideration to sexual behavior, including describing how various states and behavior could be determined from the stars, i.e., whether a woman was a virgin or had proclivities toward prostitution or homosexuality.

688. ——. "William of Saliceto on Human Sexuality." *Viator* 12 (1981): 163-81.

Describes the work of a late thirteenth-century writer who was an eminent figure at the medical school of Bologna at the time dissection was renewed in the West. He wrote *Surgery* and *Summa Conservationis et Curationis*, which is particularly detailed in its genital studies. Lemay gives a fine summary of this interesting tract that deals with (among other things) penis size and problems (including how to increase its size for intercourse), coitus (including explicit instructions on how to increase pleasure for both participants), sterility and lesbianism.

689. Leonhardt, W. "Die Homosexualität in der ältesten deutschen Dichtkunst." *Jahrbuch für sexuelle Zwischenstufen* 12 (1912): 153-65.

Argues that we do not have more examples of early German poetry about male homosexuality and bisexuality because so much of the literature in general did not survive, and this scarcity should not be used to suggest that homosexuality did not exist.

690. Lesky, E. "Die Samentheorie in der Hippokratischen Schriftensammlung." *Festschrift Max Neuburger.* Vienna: W. Maudrich, 1948, pp. 302-7.

Summarizes the different theories of the origin of sperm that were influential in the Middle Ages.

691. Leupin, Alexandre. "Le Sexe dans la langue: la dévoration." *Poétique* 45 (1981): 91-110.

Analyzes the poetic structure and sexual language of a thirteenth-century fabliau by Gautier le Leu.

692. Levy, R. "L'allusion à la sodomie dans Eneas." *Philological Quarterly* 27 (1948): 372-76.

Describes the accusation of sodomy and homosexuality made against Eneas in the twelfth-century romance.

693. Little, Lester K. "The Personal Development of Peter Damian." *Order and Innovation in the Middle Ages*. Edited by W. C. Jordan. Princeton: Princeton University Press, 1976, pp. 317-42.

Offers a brief biography of Peter Damian that attempts to explain his vehement attacks on homosexuality by recreating his early development. The conclusions are tentative, but based on strong historical analysis.

694. Loomis, C. Grant. "Three Cases of Vaginism." *Bulletin of the History of Medicine* 7 (1939): 97-98.

Describes three saints' lives in which pairs of sinners are unable to separate after intercourse. Argues that these represent instances of the medical condition of vaginism. Modern medicine finds such a phenomenon of entrapped penis impossible, so this article might be better understood as an example of sexual fear described in Hays (item 397).

695. Lorcin, Marie-Thérèse. "La Prostituée des fabliaux est-elle Intégrée ou exclue?" *Exclus et Systems d'Exclusion dans la Littérature et la Civilisations Médiévales: Acts du Colloque Organisé par le C.U.E.R.M.A. Aix-en-Provence, les 4-5-6, Mars 1977.* Series: Senefiance no. 5. Aix-en-Provence: Edition CUERMA, 1978, pp. 107-18.

Considers whether the treatment of prostitutes in literature (particularly in fabliaux) parallels that observed by historians studying legal approaches to prostitution. Concludes that in literature, prostitutes inspire fear, and are seriously excluded from society, requiring miraculous intervention for their redemption.

696. Lowes, Livingstone. "The Loveres Maladye of Hereos." *Modern Philology* 11 (1913-14): 491-546.

Clarifies Chaucer's use of the term "hereos" in the "Knight's Tale" by showing his debt to medical tracts that describe the malady of obsessive love.

697. MacKechnie, Hector. "Ius Primus Noctae." *Juridical Review* 43 (1930): 303-11.

Argues that in parts of Scotland there existed the tradition that a lord had the right to deflower virgins on their wedding night. See Howarth, item 650, who disputes the existence of this practice.

698. Mahé, J.P. "Le Sens des Symboles Sexuels dans quelques textes Hermétiques et Gnostiques." *Les Textes de Nag Hammadi.* Edited by J.E. Ménard. Leiden: Brill, 1975, pp. 123-45.

Studies the sexual symbolism in a fragment of *Discours Parfait* (*Apocalypse of Asclépius*). Argues that the essential point of this text is that the union between male and female is a sacred mystery, and that sexuality is portrayed in a more "optimistic" light than in many gnostic/dualist texts. Maintains further that this reveals there were two types of gnosticism, distinguished by their differing views on sexuality.

699. Makowski, Elizabeth. "The Conjugal Debt and Medieval Canon Law." *Journal of Medieval History* 3 (1977): 99-114.

Summarizes the canonists' struggle with conflicting views of sexuality, for example, payment of the marital debt is a positive act for the non-initiating partner, provided s/he does not enjoy it. For a fuller treatment of the subject, see Brundage, item 323.

700. Malina, Bruce. "Does Porneia mean Fornication?" *Novum Testamentum* 14 (1972): 10-17.

Examines the use of the word "porneia" in the Old and New Testaments and argues that the word only refers to "unlawful" sexual conduct, or that which is prohibited by Torah. So he concludes "pre-betrothal, pre-marital, non-commercial, heterosexual intercourse is not forbidden." He seems unduly eager to remove the biblical authority for such prohibitions. See Joseph Jensen's refutation, item 659.

701. Manuli, Paola. "Elogio della Castità: La *Ginecologia* di Sorano." *Memoria Revista di Storia delle Donne* 3 (1982): 39-49.

702. Marchello-Nizia, Christiane. "Amour Courtois, Société Masculine et Figures de Pouvoir." *Annales ESC* 6 (1981): 969-82.

Argues that the courtly love tradition, particularly as expressed in *Tristan* and *Lancelot and Guinevere*, reveals a displaced homosexual desire between the men in the love triangle. The hypothesis is both controversial and unconvincing.

703. ———. "Entre Oedipe et Carnaval: La Manekine." *Philippe de Beaumanoir, La Manekine: Roman du XIIIe Siècle* (item 155), pp. 251-72.

Analyzes the romance, *La Manekine*, describing the Oedipal qualities of the tale. A thought-provoking argument.

704. Markey, T. "Nordic Níthvísur. An Instance of Ritual Inversion?" *Mediaeval Scandinavia* 5 (1972): 7-18.

Maintains that the Nordic word, "*Níth*," is a "ritual expression of status reversal," an insult to manliness, and a sexual insult.

705. Matter, E. Ann. "My Sister, My Spouse: Woman Identified Women in Medieval Christianity." *Journal of Feminist Studies in Religion* 2,2 (Fall 1986): 81-93.

Analyzes several thirteenth-century love poems written by and to women to argue for the existence of "passionate love between women in the Middle Ages." Also considers the official attitudes towards lesbian relationships by looking at penitentials and other religious sources.

706. Matthews, William. "The Wife of Bath and All Her Sect." *Viator* 5 (1974): 413-43.

Examines the literary tradition of "randy old women" such as Chaucer's Wife of Bath. Considers medieval perceptions of sexuality in old age.

707. Mazzotti, C. "Il celibato e la castità del clero in S. Pier Damiano." *Studi su S. Pier Damiano in onore de Cardinale Amleto*. Faenza: Giovanni Cicognani. Bib. Car. Caetano Cicognani, 1970, pp. 121-32.

Summarizes Peter Damian's view on clerical celibacy, and includes a list and discussion of the tracts in which these opinions appear. These tracts are important in establishing the influential cleric's view of sexuality, and this brief article is a good starting point.

708. McAlpine, Monica E. "The Pardoner's Homosexuality and How it Matters." *Publications of the Modern Language Association* 95 (1980): 8-22.

Argues that Chaucer's characterization of the Pardoner as a "mare" means a homosexual, and that the allusion would have raised a complex interaction of images - effeminacy, hermaphroditism, and eunuchery - in the minds of the fourteenth-century audience.

709. McGuire, Brian. "Love, Friendship & Sex in the 11th Century: The Experience of Anselm." *Studia Theologica* 28 (1974): 111-52.

Investigates the life of Anselm of Bec (1033-1109), and attempts to understand Anselm's views of love, sex and friendship in the light of his personal experiences. The evidence is taken from Eadmer's *Life of St. Anselm* and Anselm's letters. The article shows the unresolved tension between Anselm's desire for friendship and his fear of sexuality.

710. Meeks, Wayne. "Image of the Androgyne: Some Uses of a Symbol in Earliest Christianity." *History of Religions* 3 (February 1974): 165-208.

Sees the origin of Christian transvestism in the Pauline writings which contain images of loss of gender difference after baptism. This argument is suggestive, but not sufficient, for, among other things, it does not address the question of why women cross-dressed and men, for the most part, did not.

711. Méla, Charles. "*Perceval*." *Yale French Studies* 55/56 (1977): 253-79.

Interprets the Perceval romance as an Oedipal myth. The argument is not well developed, and this English translation of the original French detracts from the clarity of the presentation.

712. Meyvaert, P. "Le *Libellus Responsionum* à Augustín de Cantorbéry: Une Oeuvre Authentique de Saint Grégoire le Grand." *Grégoire le Grand: Colloques Internationaux du Centre National de*

Recherche Scientifique. Paris: Éditions du CNRS, 1986, pp. 543-49.

Discusses the letter by Gregory the Great to Augustine of Canterbury which outlines Gregory's views on sex.

713. Micha, A. "Le marí jaloux dans la littérature romanesque des XIIe et XIIIe siècles." *Studi Medievali* XVII (1951): 303-20.

Studies the treatment of jealousy in twelfth and thirteenth-century French romances. Argues that jealousy naturally became an important theme in literature preoccupied with love, and considers the various ways jealousy was depicted.

714. Miller, B.D.H. "She Who Hath Drunk any Potion." *Medium Aevum* 31: 188-93.

Reviews in detail legislation about and references to abortion in medieval documents from laws, Visigothic to Justinian's Digest, to literary references, such as Chaucer.

715. Miller, Robert P. "Chaucer's Pardoner, the Scriptural Eunuch, and the Pardoner's Tale." *Speculum* 30 (1955): 180-99.

Maintains that the Parson is a scriptural "eunuch," i.e., chaste, in contrast to the Pardoner, a congenital eunuch.

716. Moller, Herbert. "The Meaning of Courtly Love." *Journal of American Folklore* 73 (1960): 39-52.

Offers a psychological interpretation of the meaning of courtly love. Argues that it was a collective fantasy caused by an infantile mother fixation. This approach was further developed by Koenigsberg, item 676.

717. Moore, Thomas. "Declining Nude." *Corona* 3: 78-82.

Reflects upon sexual and scatological illustrations in the margins of a medieval grammar book (described by Gehl, item 624), and considers the appropriate relationship between grammar and obscenity. A light essay rather than a scholarly work.

718. Murray, Alexander. "Religion among the Poor in Thirteenth-Century France." *Traditio* 30 (1974) 285-324.

Studies the sermons of Humbert de Romans, a thirteenth-century Dominican Friar, to the poor in France. Humbert reprimanded the married and unmarried for sexual improprieties, and he descried public prostitution as well as the activities of those who were "amateurs" to the trade.

719. Murray, Jacqueline. "Trial by Congress." *Lawyers Weekly* (March 27,1987): 20-1, 31.

Introduces the medieval jurists' problem of determining whether a marriage should be annulled on the grounds of impotence. Describes several of the means by which impotence was ascertained, including physical examination, medical tests, and testing by women wise in such matters. Uses trial records to illuminate a little-studied problem and its medieval solutions.

720. Mussetter, Sally. "Ritornare a lo suo principio: Dante and the Sin of Brunetto Latini." *Philological Quarterly* 63 (1984): 431-48.

Agrees with Kay (item 669) that Brunetto was not a homosexual, but claims that Dante condemned him for the sterility of his teachings.

721. Nabielek, Rainer. "Sexualerziehung im Werk des Avicenna." *NTM Schriftenriehe für Geschichte der Naturwissenschaft, Technik und Medizin* 13/2 (1976): 82-7.

722. Nelli, René. "La Continence Cathare." *Mystique et Continence* (1952): 139-51.

723. Noble, H.D. "Comment la Volonté excite ou Réfrène la Passion?" *Revue des Sciences Philosophiques et Théologiques* 17 (1928): 383-404.

724. ——. "La Moralité de la Passion." *Revue des Sciences Philosophiques et Théologiques* 20 (1931): 259-75.

725. ———. "Le Péché de Passion." *Revue Thomiste* 13 (1930): 329-53.

Discusses the sin of passion in Thomistic theology, its characteristics of suspending reason and introducing physiological turmoil. Further considers such questions as when one must assume responsibility for passion, the physical versus psychological dimensions of passion, the varying degrees of culpability for acts done from passion or habit.

726. Nodet, Charles-Henri. "Position de Saint Jérôme en face des Problèmes Sexueles." *Mystique et Continence* (1952): 308-56.

727. Noonan, John T. "Marital Affection in the Canonists." *Studia Gratiana* 12 (1967): 479-509.

Argues that Gratian and the Decretals taught that "marital affection" sufficed to constitute a valid marriage. In the course of the argument, Noonan explains how intercourse was affected by feelings of marital affection in the eyes of the church.

728. Noury, Paul. "Adam et Eve dans l'Art Religieux Normand et les Livres d'Anatomie." *La Chronique Médicale* ix no. 22 (1902): 741-46.

Shows that some fifteenth-century nude representations of Adam and Eve were based on contemporary anatomy texts.

729. O'Meara, John J. "Virgil and S. Augustine: The Roman Background to Christian Sexuality." *Augustinus* 13/52 (1968): 307-26.

Demonstrates Augustine's debt to Virgil for some ideas on sexuality (for example the weakening and destructive aspects of intercourse), and argues that Virgil exerted a strong influence on Augustine and through him, on subsequent western theology.

730. Otis, Leah Lydia. "Prostitution and Repentance in Late Medieval Perpignan." *Women of the Medieval World*. Edited by J. Kirshner and S. Wemple. Oxford: Basil Blackwell, 1985, pp. 137-60.

Presents a preliminary survey that is covered more fully in Otis' book on the subject, item 460.

731. Paden, William D. "Utrum Copularentur: Of Cors." *L'Esprit Createur* 19 (1979): 70-83.

Raises the question of whether troubadour poetry involved sexual fulfillment, but fails to answer it, concluding that the evidence is insufficient to decide. In the course of the discussion, the author recounts erotic references and double entendres in the troubadour poems.

732. Padgug, Robert A. "Sexual Matters: On Conceptualizing Sexuality in History." *Radical History Review* 20 (1979): 3-23.

Presents a thoughtful general survey of the problem of studying the history of sexuality. While it does not deal directly with the Middle Ages, it raises important methodological considerations.

733. Patlagean, Evelyne. "L'Histoire de la Femme Déguisée en Moine et l'évolution de la Sainteté Féminine à Byzance." *Studi Medievale* ser. 3, 17 (1976): 597-623.

Analyzes the hagiographic tradition of transvestite saints, and shows that the stories all speak of overturning a social order based on gender. Includes a list of female transvestite saints with locations of editions of their *Vitae*.

734. Patterson, Lee. "For the Wyves Love of Bathe: Feminine Rhetoric and Poetic Resolution in the *Roman de la Rose* and the *Canterbury Tales*." *Speculum* 58 (1983): 656-95.

Traces the association between language, garrulousness, and sexuality in medieval literature, particularly but not limited to the Wife of Bath's Tale and the *Roman de la Rose*, then explores the sexual revelations in the structure of Chaucer's tale.

735. Pavan, Elizabeth. "Police des moeurs, société et politique à Venise à la fin du moyen âge." *Revue Historique* 264 (1980): 241-88.

Analyzes prostitution and sodomy in the fourteenth century, including changes in attitudes and practices. A perceptive article that not only details changes in practice, but offers an hypothesis as to why such changes occurred.

736. Payer, Pierre J. "Early Medieval Regulations Concerning Marital Sex Relations." *Journal of Medieval History* 6 (1980): 353-76.

Traces the development of rules to regulate legitimate marital intercourse -- particularly positions and frequency. Based mainly on the penitentials and covers the period from the sixth through the eleventh centuries. An excellent survey, but superceded by Payer's book on the subject, item 468.

737. ——. "Foucault on Penance and the Shaping of Sexuality." *Studies in Religion/Sciences Religieuses* 14 (1985): 313-20.

Disputes Foucault's (item 377) contention that the Fourth Lateran Council's requirement of annual confession caused an increase in sexual repression. Payer notes that sexual behavior received relatively less attention in the penitentials after 1215 than it had before.

738. Pereira, Michela. "Maternità e sessualità femminile in Ildegarda di Bingen: Proposte de lettura." *Quaderni storici* 44 (8/1980): 564-79.

Analyzes Hildegard of Bingen's medical tract to consider her view that the enjoyment of sex was a prerequisite for the generation of healthy children. Compare this article with those of Cadden, item 579, and Scholz, item 776.

739. Perret, Michèle. "Travesties et Transsexuelles: Yde, Silence, Grisandole, Blanchandine." *Romance Notes* 25,3 (Spring 1985): 328-40.

Studies the occurrences of female transvestites and transsexuals in four French romances of the thirteenth and fourteenth centuries.

740. Pharr, Mary Brown. "The Kiss in Roman Law." *The Classical Journal* 42 (1946/47): 393-97.

Studies the significance of the kiss in Roman Law for ceremonies, betrothal, and as a contract, and looks at select examples of the continuation of these practices into the Middle Ages, particularly in Visigothic law. The article is brief and the subject deserves fuller treatment.

741. Pigeaud, J. "Le Rêve érotique dans l'Antiquité grèco-romain: l'oneirogmos." *Littérature, Médecine, Société* 3 (1981): 10-11.

742. Pinto, Lucille B. "The folk practice of gynecology and obstetrics in the Middle Ages." *Bulletin of the History of Medicine* 47 (1973): 513-23.

Studies Latin manuscript codex 803 of Burgerbibliothek in Bern, Switzerland, and describes the intertwining of folk remedies and "school medicine" for problems with childbirth, menstruation, and contraception.

743. Pittaluga, Stéfano. "Alano di Lilla e la Rimula Veneris." *Maia* 31 (1979): 147-50.

Explicates one of the double-entendres in Alan of Lille's *The Plaint of Nature*. More helpful is the fuller work by Jan Ziolkowski, item 526.

744. Pizarro, J.M. "On Níth against Bishops." *Mediaeval Scandinavia* 11 (1982): 149-53.

Discusses four incidents in historical sources of insults directed against bishops that accused the bishops of unmanliness by implying they take a passive role in homosexual encounters. Further maintains these incidents fall within a long-standing Germanic tradition of such insults.

745. Plucknett, T.F.T. "Chaucer's Escapade." *Law Quarterly Review* 64 (1948): 33-63.

Disputes Watts' (item 809) claim that Chaucer's friends were involved in Cecilia's rape.

746. Porteau-Bitker, Annik. "Criminalité et délinquance féminines dans le droit pénal des XIIIe et XIVe siècles." *Revue Historique de Droit Français et étranger* 58 (1980): 13-56.

Studies women criminals in thirteenth and fourteenth-century France, and since the most common crimes for which women were prosecuted were prostitution, adultery, and acting as a procuress, the article makes a solid contribution to study of those subjects.

747. Post, J.B. "Ravishment of Women and the Statutes of Westminster." *Legal Records and the Historian*. Edited by John H. Baker. London: Royal Historical Society 1978, pp. 150-64.

Analyzes two statutes of Westminster from the thirteenth century against rape and shows that the trend was not to protect women against rape, but to protect family interests against elopement. The article reproduces the Statutes themselves as an appendix.

748. ———. "Ages at Menarche and Menopause: Some Medieval Authorities." *Population Studies* 25 (1971): 83-87.

Studies medical texts and determines that medieval menarche took place between 12 and 15 years old. However, he disregards the same sources that place the age of menopause between 50 and 60. This selectivity calls his conclusions into question.

749. Powers, James F. "Frontier Municipal Baths and Social Interaction in Thirteenth Century Spain." *American Historical Review* 84 (1979): 649-59.

Studies bath-houses in thirteenth-century Spain and discusses the legislation surrounding them. The laws mention rape, prostitution and voyeurism, but this article does not address these issues in any meaningful way. The author is interested in the interaction between Muslim, Jew and Christian in the bath. Nevertheless, the laws represent a fruitful area of research on sexuality.

750. Quilligan, Maureen. "Words and Sex: The Language of Allegory in the *De Planctu Naturae,* the *Roman de la Rose*...." *Allegorica* 2 (1977): 195-216.

Considers the relationship between language and sexuality arguing for the importance of the former in shaping the attitudes toward the latter. Studies three texts that reveal this: *De Planctu Naturae*, *The Romance of the Rose* and Spencer's *Fairie Queen*.

751. Reinhard, J. R. "Burning at the Stake in Medieval Law and Literature." *Speculum* 16 (1941): 186-209.

Examines the incidences in the romances of burning at the stake as a penalty for adultery, and looks at early Germanic and Celtic law codes to find the origins of the punishment. Concludes that the authors of the romances got the idea not from Germanic precedent, but from Old Testament biblical law.

752. Rendle, W. "The Stews on Bankside." *The Antiquarian Magazine and Bibliographer* 2.8 (August 1882): 70-77.

Summarizes the medieval regulations of London's prostitution district of Southwark. Although the author apologizes for his topic, he nevertheless offers a guide to manuscript sources on the subject.

753. Revard, Carter. "The Tow on Absalom's distaff and the Punishment of Lechers in Medieval England." *English Language Notes* 17 (1980): 168-70.

Considers the meaning of the phrase "to have tow on one's distaff" (used by Absalom in Chaucer's "Miller's Tale") and shows that to carry a distaff with tow on it was statutory punishment for persons guilty of crimes of sex and violence.

754. Roberti, Melchiorre. "'Delictum' e 'peccatum' nelle fonti romane e cristiane." *Studi di Storia e Diritto in Onore di Carlo Calisse vol. 1* Milan: A. Guiffre, 1940, pp. 159-76.

755. Roby, Douglas. "Early Medieval Attitudes toward Homosexuality." *Gai Saber* 1 (1977): 67-79.

Intends to describe the history of attitudes toward homosexuality, but this dated work has been superceded by the work of Boswell, item 310.

756. Rolleston, J.D. "Penis Captivus: A Historical Note." *Janus* 39 (1936): 196-201.

Recounts incidents from medieval texts that describe the occurrence of a medical condition the author calls "penis captivus," or "incarceration of the organ in the vagina due to psycho-genic spasmodic contraction of the levator ani...." Modern medicine denies the existence of such a condition. See Hays (item 397) for a discussion of the kinds of sexual fears that lead to such analysis.

757. Ross, Margaret Clunies. "An Interpretation of the myth of Þorr's encounter with Geirrodr and his daughters." *Speculum Norroenum*. Edited by Ursula Dronke, *et al.* Odense: Odense University Press, 1981, pp. 370-91.

Maintains that the symbolism in the *Þórsdrápa* expresses sexual struggles that include the power of women's menstrual blood and urination as an expression of sexual dominance.

758. ———. "Concubinage in Anglo-Saxon England." *Past and Present* 108 (1985): 3-34.

Analyzes concubinage as a marriage pattern, demonstrating that it existed in Anglo-Saxon England. Also includes a summary of varying penalties for adultery and rape.

759. Rossiaud, Jacques. "Prostitution, Youth, and Society in the Towns of Southeastern France in the Fifteenth Century." *Deviants and the Abandoned in French Society*. Edited by Robert Forster. Baltimore: Johns Hopkins University Press, 1978, pp. 1-46.

Argues convincingly that prostitution in the Middle Ages was more tolerated and integrated into the whole fabric of society than it would be later after the Reformation.

760. Roth, Norman. "'Deal gently with the young man': Love of Boys in Medieval Hebrew Poetry of Spain." *Speculum* 57,1 (January 1982): 20-51.

Analyzes Hebrew love poems from twelfth-century Spain. Some are quite explicit in their references to homosexual activity, while most are more courtly in their approach to love. This diversity has led to disputes about whether homosexual activities actually took place in Spanish Jewish communities. Roth argues that the poems were not just allegorical.

761. ——. "Satire and Debate in Two Famous Medieval Poems from al-Andalus." *The Maghreb Review* 4 (1979): 105-13.

Translates two poems by eleventh-century Hebrew poets which contain homosexual eroticism. Roth's accompanying analysis is scholarly and lucid.

762. Rowland, Beryl. "Animal Imagery and the Pardoner's Abnormality." *Neophilologus* 48 (1964): 56-60.

Argues that Chaucer's associations of the Pardoner with a hare and a goat comment on the Pardoner's sexuality, since both animals were considered hermaphroditic and lascivious.

763. ——. "Chaucer's Idea of the Pardoner." *Chaucer Review* 14 (1979): 140-54.

Provides background on medieval notions of hermaphroditism to argue that the Pardoner was one.

764. Roy, Bruno. "André le Chapelain ou l'obscenité rendue courtoise." *Coll. Wurzburg 1984, Mittelalter Bilder aus neuer Perspektive, Diskussions Anstosse zu "Amour Courtois", Subjektivitat in der Dichtung und Strategien des Erzahlens.* Edited by P. Ruhe and R. Dehrens. Munich: W. Fink, 1985, pp. 253-54.

Develops the same argument as Betsy Bowden, item 556.

765. ——. "La Belle e(s)t la bête, Aspects du bestiare feminin au Moyen Age." *Etudes Françaises* 10 (1974): 320-34.

Considers the view of women portrayed in medieval bestiaries. Among other associations, he shows how women, like beasts, were associated with sexuality.

766. Ruggiero, G. "Sexual Criminality in the Early Renaissance: Venice 1338-1358." *Journal of Social History* 8 (1975): 18-37.

Studies perceptions of rape in fourteenth-century Venice by analyzing the punishments enforced. Demonstrates, among other things, the peculiar fact that rape was not taken very seriously, although sodomy was punished very severely. The article also covers other kinds of sexual crimes. Well researched, well argued, with useful notes.

767. Russell, Jeffrey Burton and Mark W. Wyndham. "Witchcraft and the Demonization of Heresy." *Mediaevalia* 2 (1976): 1-21.

Maintains sexual orgy was one of the chief identifying characteristics of witchcraft by the fifteenth century, and it derived not from any particular heresy, but from a tradition that had accused heretics in general of such practices throughout the Middle Ages. Traces the development and religious significance of orgies from the ancient world through the Middle Ages.

768. Saenger, Paul. "Silent Reading: Its impact on Late Medieval Script and Society." *Viator* 13 (1982): 367-414.

Presents a scholarly and important analysis tracing the transformation of a tradition of oral reading, which started in the classical world, to silent reading, which slowly took over the medieval monasteries from the end of the twelfth to the fourteenth centuries, then spread to the laity. The author includes one section suggesting that by the end of the fifteenth century, the intimacy of silent reading permitted more graphic expressions of sexuality in religious literature (naked miniatures in books of hours, for example) and sexual escapades to be recorded. The argument for inclusion of sexual materials in books produced for silent reading needs more evidence. Many "public" fora (i.e., the Bayeux tapestry) contain nudity.

769. Sagmüller, Johannes Baptista. "Das 'Impedimentum impotentiae' bei der Frau vor Alexander III." *Theologische Quartalschrift* 93 (1911): 90-126.

770. ——. "Nochmals das 'Impedimentum impotentiae' bei der Frau vor Alexander III." *Theologische Quartalschrift* 95 (1913): 565-611.

771. Salisbury, Joyce E. "The Latin Doctors of the Church on Sexuality." *Journal of Medieval History* 12 (1986): 279-89.

Argues there were two principal patristic views of sexuality that influenced the West. One was a fundamentally dualistic view that saw all sexual activity as evil, and the Augustinian view which saw sexual intercourse as theoretically good and natural, but polluted by lust, a characteristic of sexuality in a fallen world.

772. Sastre Santos, E. "Sobre el aforismo, 'Adulter est in sum uxorem amator ardentior' allegado en el Decreto C. 32q.4c.5." *Apollinaris* 57 (1984): 587-626.

773. Schirmann, Jefim. "The Ephebe in Medieval Hebrew Poetry." *Sefarad* 15 (1955): 54-68.

Studies Hebrew pederastic poetry in Moslem Spain that was influenced by Arabic poetry on similar themes. See also, Norman Roth's more recent article on the subject, item 760.

774. Schnapp, Jeffrey T. "Dante's Sexual Solecisms: Gender and Genre in the *Commedia*." *Romanic Review* 79,1 (January 1988): 143-63.

Argues that the medieval tradition provided two approaches to gender inversions: a completely negative one, articulated by Alan of Lille as "unnatural" and homosexual, and a positive religious one that could see Jesus as feminine and female saints with beards. Further maintains that Dante incorporated both in the *Comedy*.

775. Schnell, Rüdiger. "Ovids Ars Amatoria und die höfische Minnetheorie." *Euphorion* 69 (1975: 132-59.

Studies medieval poetry to discover the underlying moral standards articulated in the literature. In the process, he contrasts the theories of love of Ovid, Andreas Capellanus, Konrad von Würzburg, and others.

776. Scholz, Bernhard W. "Hildegard von Bingen on the Nature of Woman." *American Benedictine Review* 31 (1980): 361-83.

Summarizes Hildegard's views of women, including her views on sexuality. The author notes that although Hildegard accepted many medieval misogynist views, she was not influenced by Aristotle's medical opinions, so her view of sexuality was more positive than his. For a fuller treatment of Hildegard's view of sex, see Cadden, item 579.

777. Schroter, Michael. "Staatsbildung und Triebkontrolle:zur gesellschaftlichen Regulierung des Sexualverhaltens ..." *Amsterdams Sociologisch Tijdschrift*, 8 (May 1981): 48-90.

778. Segalla, G. "I Cataloghi dei peccati in S. Paolo." *Studia Patavina* 15 (1968): 205-28.

Presents an excellent background of biblical scholarship to supplement medieval studies of the theology of Paul.

779. Selvin, Rhoda Hurwitt. "Shades of Love in the *Parlement of Foules*." *Studia Neophilologica* 37 (1965): 146-60.

Argues unconvincingly that Chaucer wrestled with the problem of how to reconcile "worldly love," which is sexual, with the teaching of the Church. Concludes that the comments on love by the birds in the tale do not effect a resolution of the problem.

780. Shaw, James Rochester. "Scientific Empiricism in the Middle Ages: Albertus Magnus on Sexual Anatomy and Physiology." *Clio Medica* 10 (1975): 53-64.

Claims that Albert the Great had a commitment to an empirical approach, particularly in sexual matters. Notes where Albert departed from Aristotle (i.e., in the addition of a "psychology of sexual arousal"), and from Constantine the African (omitting his remedies for impotence and prolonging intercourse). The author's proof for "modern empiricism" may not be fully proven, but his summary of Albert's analysis of sexuality is concise, clear, and useful.

781. Silagi, Gabriel. "Ein pedantischer Liebesbrief aus dem 14. Jahrhundert." *Archiv fur Kulturgeschichte* 51 (1969): 234-62.

782. Silvestre, Hubert. "Rupert de Deutz et John Boswell désarmes devant la même devinette." *Revue d'histoire ecclésiastique* 80 (1985): 771-75.

Disputes Boswell's suggestion that "wood" in Rupert's riddle refers to masturbation or homosexuality. Of course, this must be read in conjunction with Boswell, item 310.

783. Smith, Cyril J. "History of Rape and Rape Laws." *Women Lawyers Journal* 60 (1974): 188-91.

Summarizes laws against rape in the Code of Hammurabi, ancient Hebrew laws, and English Common Law, and compares them with the modern common law definition of rape. The article treats rape as if it were the same throughout history, so it does not consider medieval views and variations (for example, "rape" with consent as a way to avoid parental consent for marriage).

784. Sogner, Sølvi. "Allaitement au sein et abstinence sexuelle au moyen âge." *Annales de Démographie Historique* (1986/87): 353-59.

Proposes to explain the eleventh- or twelfth-century Norwegian Law that requires women to end breast feeding by arguing that the Church had an interest both in preventing sexual relations during lactation, but also in restoring a woman sexually to her husband by shortening the nursing period.

785. Spencer, Richard. "The treatment of Women in the *Roman de la Rose*, the *Fabliaux* and the *Quinze Joyes de Mariage*." *Marche Romane* 28 (1978): 207-14.

Maintains that the works are not as anti-feminist as some might think. Argues that by portraying sexual instincts and activities as natural and desirable, these works restored an equality to men and women that was lacking in the courtly tradition.

786. Stanley-Jones, D. "Sexual Inversion and the English Law." *The Medical Press and Circular* 215, no. 5588 (June 12, 1946): 391-98.

Argues that the thirteenth-century controversy over Aristotle and Averroës at the University of Paris was a hidden struggle over homosexuality.

787. Stefanutti, Ugo. "Venetian Courtesans of Bygone Times." *Rass Medica* 36, 3: 153-68.

788. Stehling, Thomas. "To Love a Medieval Boy." *Journal of Homosexuality* 8 (1983): 151-70.

Discusses the flourishing of homosexual poetry during the twelfth-century renaissance and analyzes some of the poetry of Marbod, Baudri and Hilary the Englishman to consider some of the themes explored by such poetry. Compares descriptions of boys and girls in love poetry and notes the importance of classical models for expressions of homosexual love.

789. Stillwell, Gardiner. "The Language of Love in Chaucer's Miller's and Reeve's Tales and in the Old French Fabliaux." *Journal of English and Germanic Philology* 54 (1955): 693-99.

Claims that "the use of would-be elegant love-diction in ironic contexts was well established in fabliaux literature long before Chaucer's time." Serves as a guide to some of the fabliaux that have sexual themes similar to those identified in Chaucer.

790. Stone, Lawrence. "Sex in the West: The Strange History of Human Sexuality." *The New Republic* (July 8, 1985): 25-37.

Notes that until the mid-1970's, the study of sexuality had been dominated by sociologists, psychologists, and sexologists, but had been neglected by historians. Surveys some of the historical work on the subject (notably that of Foucault, item 377, Boswell, item 310, Otis, item 460, Ariés, item 295, Brown, item 321, and Roy, item 489) to argue that sexuality is a "cultural artifact that has undergone constant...change."

791. Storm, Melvin. "The Pardoner's Invitation: Questor's Bag or Beckett's Shrine." *Publications of the Modern Language Association*, 97 (1982): 810-18.

Continues the discussion of the Pardoner's sexuality (see for example, Rowland, and Miller), concentrating not on the Pardoner's sexual inclinations, but on equating pilgrimage with sexual intercourse and clerical corruption with sodomy.

792. Stow, Kenneth. "The Jewish Family in the Rhineland in the High Middle Ages: Form and Function." *American Historical Review* 92, 5 (1987): 1085-110.

Includes a full discussion of medieval Judaic views on sexuality, including specific sexual acts, with excellent notes that guide one to the Jewish sources.

793. Terroine, Anne. "Le Roi des Ribauds de l'Hôtel du Roi et les Prostituées Parisiennes." *Revue Historique de Droit Français et Étranger* 56 (1978):253-67.

Introduces a fragment of a document dated 1417, which shows that Parisian prostitutes came under the jurisdiction of a particular officer in the royal household. Discusses the general duties of the "*roi des ribauds*," including his responsibility for prostitutes.

794. Thomasset, Claude. "La Femme au Moyen Age. Les Composantes fondamentales de sa répresentation: immunité-impunité." *Ornicar* 22-23 (1981): 83-4.

Analyzes the medieval belief that women can become immune to poison and yet poison others. This belief contributed to men's fear of menstruation and venereal disease.

795. Thorndike, Lynn. "Further Consideration of the *Experimenta, Speculum Astronomiae,* and *De Secretis Mulierum* ascribed to Albertus Magnus." *Speculum* 30 (1955): 413-43.

Compares the *De Secretis Mulierum* (item 245) with Albert's position on sexuality and generation in other works to argue that the *De Secretis* was not composed by Albert, but that much of it was taken from his authentic works. Reconsiders Ferckel's (item 616) assessment of the tract.

796. Tobin, Frank. "Concupiscentia and Courtly Love." *Romance Notes* 14 (1972): 387-92.

Maintains that a tradition of courtly love that accepted sexual intercourse outside of marriage was a logical consequence of a society that did not wholly accept sex within marriage. Draws from Augustinian views on sex and marriage and Andreas Capellanus' views on love.

797. Tomasson, Richard F. "Premarital Sexual Permissiveness and Illegitimacy in the Nordic Countries." *Comparative Studies in Society and History* 18 (1976): 252-70.

Argues that Iceland's high rate of illegitimacy in modern times derives from a continuity of casual sexual behavior from the medieval period. Describes some medieval sources that mention Icelandic sexual amorality, but the argument for continuity is not fully convincing.

798. Toubert, P. "La Théorie du Mariage chez les Moralistes Carolingens." *Il Matrimonio nella Societa Altomedievale*. Spoleto: Centro Italiano, 1976, pp. 233-85.

799. Vaca, César. "La Sexualidad en San Agustin." *Augustinus Magister*. Edited by Congrès International Augustinien. Paris: Etudes Augustiniennes, 1954, pp. 727-36.

Compares Augustine's reflections on sex with Freud's, noting differences and similarities. He considers five issues (chosen because they lend themselves to Freudian comparison). These issues are the sexual instinct, infantile sexuality, adolescent sexuality, repression of sexuality and marital sex. While the material on Augustine is generally accurate, the comparison between the two is not particularly useful, since he concludes that there are more differences than similarities between them.

800. Vance, Eugene. "Le Combat érotique chez Chrétien de Troyes: De la figure à la forme." *Poétique* 3 (1972): 544-71.

Reviews the conjunction of erotic experience with combat in war that is a constant theme in the imagination of the West. Argues that Chrétien was influential in transmitting this tradition.

801. Vereecke, L. "Marriage et sexualité au declin du moyen âge." *Supplément de la Vie Spirituelle* 57 (1961): 199-225.

802. Villard, François. "Guillaume IX d'Aquitaine et le Concile de Reims de 1119." *Cahiers de Civilisation Médiévale* 16 (1973): 295-302.

Describes the adulterous behavior of William IX, Count of Poitiers.

803. Vinay, Gustavo. "Il '*De Amore*' di Andrea Cappellano nel quadro della letteratura amorosa e della Rinascita del Secolo XII." *Studi Medievali* n.s. 17 (1951): 203-76.

Provides an analysis of the *De Amore* and places the tract in its historical context.

804. von Vershuer, U.F. "Die Homosexuellen in Dantes Göttliche Komodie." *Jahrbuch für sexuelle Zwischenstufen* 8 (1906): 353-63.

805. Vorwahl, H. "Die Sexualität im Mittelalter." *Janus* 37 (1933): 293-99.

806. Wack, Mary F. "The Measure of Pleasure: Peter of Spain on Men, Women, and Lovesickness." *Viator* 17 (1986): 173-96.

Analyzes the intellectual and cultural contexts of Peter of Spain's medical text discussing lovesickness and summarizes Peter's findings. Peter's questions about which gender suffers more leads to questions about which gender enjoys intercourse more, and how one can measure such things. This article's analysis reveals much about perceptions of gender and sexuality. Contains extensive notes.

807. Wailes, Stephen L. "Students as Lovers in the German Fabliau." *Medium Aevum* 46 (1977): 196-211.

Analyzes three German fabliaux, *Studentenabentur A*, *Frauenlist*, and *Die treue Magd* to show that Germans, more than French, portrayed students as successful in seduction due to their "reputed wit and savoir-faire."

808. Walker, Sue Sheridan. "Punishing Convicted Ravishers: Statutory Strictures and Actual Practice in Thirteenth and Fourteenth Century England." *Journal of Medieval History* 13 (1987): 237-50.

Investigates English statutes that provide for stronger sanctions against ravishment and abduction than in previous centuries, and analyzes the relationship between the statutes and the actual penalties enforced. Also considers the relationship between medieval terminology and modern definitions of rape.

809. Watts, P.R. "The Strange Case of Geoffrey Chaucer and Cecilia Chaumpaigne." *Law Quarterly Review* 63 (1947): 491-515.

Maintains that Chaucer was charged with rape (not merely abduction) and includes an edition of the relevant documents. Also argues that Chaucer's friends were involved, which is disputed by Plucknett, item 745.

810. Wedek, Harry E. "Synonyms for Meretrix." *Classical Weekly* 37, No. 10 (January 1944): 116-17.

Lists Latin words (classical and Medieval) used for prostitutes, fornicators and other wanton women.

811. Westphal-Wihl, Sarah. "The Ladies' Tournament: Marriage, Sex, and Honor in Thirteenth-Century Germany." *Signs* 14 (Winter 1989): 371-98.

Argues that the thirteenth-century romance, *Der Vrouwen Turnei*, revealed transvestite activity as a challenge to patriarchal power.

812. White, Sarah Melhado. "Sexual Language and Human Conflict in Old French Fabliaux." *Comparative Studies in Society and History* 24,2 (1982): 185-210.

Argues that the fabliaux introduced a new theme into European literature: sexuality that brought "rivalrous interpersonal struggle" instead of personal fulfillment. Analyzes the use of sexual terms and tales in which genitals play an important role. A well-reasoned, thought-provoking argument.

813. Williams, Harry F. "French Fabliau Scholarship." *South Atlantic Review* 46,1 (January 1981): 76-82.

Compiles a bibliography of studies on the fabliaux, which are such an important source for attitudes on medieval sexuality.

814. Wood, Charles T. "The Doctor's Dilemma: Sin, Salvation, and the Menstrual Cycle in Medieval Thought." *Speculum* 56 (1981): 710-27.

Describes medieval medical and theological views on the menstrual cycle and its relationship to reproduction and lactation. Also considers the subtle, yet theologically difficult problem of Jesus' birth and nurturing by a virgin. An important article for getting at the medieval mentality as it struggled with the question,"Did Mary menstruate?"

815. Wright, David F. "Homosexuals or Prostitutes? The Meaning of AP ENOKO AI (1 Cor. 6:9, I Tim, 1:10) *Vigiliae Christianae* 38 (1984): 125-53.

Challenges Boswell's (item 310) claim that the biblical reference refers to male homosexuality.

INDEX

AUTHOR/EDITOR

INDEX

SUBJECT

INDEX

CENTURY
Primary Sources